House Within a House

House Within a House
Nicholas Dawson

Translated by
David Bradford

BRICK BOOKS

Library and Archives Canada Cataloguing in Publication

Title: House within a house / Nicholas Dawson ; translated by David Bradford.
Other titles: Désormais, ma demeure. English
Names: Dawson, Nicholas, 1982- author. | Bradford, David (Poet), translator.
Description: Poems. | Translation of: Désormais, ma demeure.
Identifiers: Canadiana (print) 20220489173 | Canadiana (ebook) 20220493499 | ISBN
9781771316071 (softcover) | ISBN 9781771316095 (PDF) | ISBN 9781771316088 (EPUB)
Classification: LCC PS8607.A965 D4713 2023 | DDC C841/.6—dc23

Published by arrangement with éditions Triptyque, Montreal. Originally published in French
as Désormais, ma demeure in 2020.

We gratefully acknowledge the Canada Council for the Arts, the Government of Canada
through the Canada Book Fund, and the Ontario Arts Council for their support of our
publishing program.

  Canada Council Conseil des arts
for the Arts du Canada

 ONTARIO ARTS COUNCIL
CONSEIL DES ARTS DE L'ONTARIO
an Ontario government agency
un organisme du gouvernement de l'Ontario

Government Gouvernement
of Canada du Canada

Edited by Erín Moure.
Author photo by Cedric Trahan.
Translator photo by Sarah Bodri.
The cover image is Blue Night (2018) by Matthew Wong (© Matthew Wong Foundation /
Artists Rights Society (ARS), New York / Socan).
The book is set in Adobe Caslon Pro and Avenir Next Condensed.
Design by Emma Allain.
Printed and bound by Coach House Printing.

Brick Books
487 King St. W.
Kingston, ON
K7L 2X7
www.brickbooks.ca

BRICK BOOKS

Though much of the work of Brick Books takes place on the ancestral lands of the Anishinaabeg,
Haudenosaunee, Huron-Wendat, and Mississaugas of the Credit peoples, our editors, authors,
and readers from many backgrounds are situated from coast to coast to coast in Canada on the
traditional and unceded territories of over six hundred nations who have cared for Turtle Island
from time immemorial. While living and working on these lands, we are committed to hearing
and returning the rightful imaginative space to the poetries, songs, and stories that have been
untold, under-told, wrongly told, and suppressed through colonization.

To my mother,
mami–luna viva, brillante.

You too are driven by the desire to understand, know, y saber how human and other beings know. Beneath your desire for knowledge writhes the hunger to understand and love yourself.

Gloria Anzaldúa
this bridge we call home:
radical visions for transformation

As I walk, I guess my little smile is enfolding a new thought: when I get inside maybe I'll put these words on a scrap of paper and see whether they look (as they sort of sound to me) like the possible start of a poem.

Eve Kosofsky Sedgwick
A Dialogue on Love

The way I remember it, it's not cold out, because my love and I are walking slowly down the street, because my love's hand, in the winter quiet, settles on my back, his naked hand, no glove, and I'm hoping his tenderness gives me the strength to face this family birthday dinner in my deeply depressed state, a dinner I organized myself because my sister lives in Europe, because my mother has gone off to Chile to get through her own depression, because for months this splintered family has been smothered in scandals and forbidden subjects, and I can feel this loving hand on my back through my too-thin-for-February coat: my depression's winter is a very cold one, but I don't really know it because I only leave the house when I have to, to see my therapist, my acupuncturist, my doctor, my trainer.

The way I remember it, I don't at all feel like celebrating, but I've got to because birthdays don't care about our struggles. I'm not convinced this one can be avoided all that easily, I drag it down Alexandre DeSève Street like a ball and chain, all the way to the faux-fancy French bistro, a restaurant from another time with too-high prices and a too-baroque décor, a restaurant aging poorly but still there, obstinately, amidst Ontario Street's colourful crowds. I think to myself *there's something sad about this empty resto and its stubborn faux-fancy thing*, I no longer know if I share the thought with my partner, who keeps his hand between my shoulder blades, or if I keep it to myself: maybe the sentence is less pretty, less complete, more abrupt, something like *sad faux-fancy resto*, or maybe I'm making it up as I write these lines down, because the way I remember it, my sentences are splintered like my family, loud like my nights, empty like this street and restaurant from another time, because those old sentences seem more thoughtful today, more poetic, better constructed maybe.

The way I remember it, my sister is in Europe and my mother is in Chile, my brother, with his wife and kid, hasn't arrived yet, and my father is already there, my father to whom I've barely spoken in months, who feels guilty about my state and is trying, as best he can, to redeem himself; my anger is pitiless because it's gnawing at me, eating away at me every night, so when he gives me his gift before we've even ordered, before we've even glanced at the menu, I stare it down with bad faith that my partner recognizes and rushes to tamp down with his hand on my thigh this time—and I comply, I soften my look, I say *gracias*, I unwrap the thing with a forced smile that fails to hold back the tears I feel welling up, I don't know why I'm thinking, in this exact moment, about my mother halfway around the world, mother who I'm worried about because last night I dreamt of her death, which she's been telling me about in every email she sends, once every two weeks, to ask how I'm doing and to tell me she isn't well, but this thinking about my mother making these tears well up stops abruptly when I discover what my father got me: poetry books, three books written by people unknown to him, a dead poet, an old living poet, a young poet, three books recommended by a bookseller to whom my father'd spoken of his son the poet and teacher, I tell myself he forgot to tell her that I no longer write, that I no longer teach, that I no longer read, that I spend all my days looking at the glass separating my apartment from what's outside. These books are carefully chosen, I'm moved by this gift, I see that I no longer have the right to be mad at him, which all at once upsets and saddens me, I repeat *gracias*, I believe my father hears my appreciation, my emotion, but my brother and his wife put an end to the moment by arriving late with my nephew who doesn't notice anything, who says *Tío Nicho* in his naïve, cute voice, who hops about despite the restaurant's frosty welcome, despite its baroque décor, despite its chandeliers and heavy curtains, despite the little candles on the table which my brother's wife moves out of the kid's reach with that aggressively motherly cautiousness—later, she'll ask *when are you going back to work?* Later, she'll ask *but what do you do with your days?*

The way I remember it, I don't answer anything; maybe, benevolently, my partner answers for me, aware as he is of my capacity for lashing out from the depths of my angriness. I remember thinking *I spend my days looking at the glass separating my apartment from what's outside*, I remember wanting to answer honestly *I spend hours curled up in bed, and then I crawl to the living room, and I'm unsure what comes next because I forget what I'm doing, I forget time passing, everything passes me by, everything escapes me, and lately I spend long hours taking pictures of my apartment, walking around on my knees to photograph the chair legs and baseboards, sliding along on my back to get my camera under the armchair and table, arms outstretched to photograph the dust under the couch and under the bed, producing blurry images, capturing light rather than shapes, capturing traces of the bedroom, kitchen and living room despairingly reflected off every glass surface in the place. I spend my days producing images of my confinement, images in which I confine myself.*

The way I remember it, I didn't say any of that, I'm even proud that I knew how to bite my tongue and act properly. The way I remember it, I don't blame my sister-in-law for asking such a question, I don't hold my brother's being late against him, I don't blame my father for the gifts I can't use, I don't resent anyone for avoiding, after her question, the subject of my sick leave, of my depression, of my pain and anger, and for also avoiding my mother's depression and trip to Chile. The way I remember it, I'm strong enough to realize that there's nothing to be done with a depressed person who only gets out of the house when they must. But my memories fail me: I can't tell what's true from what's not, and in the moment I write these lines I don't remember what state I was in while out of the house this time, if I had tears in my eyes or rage all over my face, if I managed to hide my urge to escape, if I talked too much or too little, if I actually heard anything said to me. The way I remember it, this time out of the house convinced me that it was still best that I keep myself shut away.

TO COME BACK TO THE PHOTOS I TOOK WHILE ILL—
there were about forty, as if thoughts taking the shape
of interior wanderings from years long since past, in the
midst of my depression but after I had come through
the hardest period, one wherein reading and writing were
impossible for me, and which Julia Kristeva calls the period

Julia Kristeva
*Soleil noir:
Dépression et
mélancolie*

that ends up *l'asymbolie, la perte de sens : si je ne suis plus
capable de traduire ou de métaphoriser, je me tais et je meurs.*[1]
I wasn't able to find my words yet, their letters jumbled in
front of me; only the image had recovered a tiny bit of its
redeeming potential, at best via its power to symbolize,
at worst via its capacity for flatly reproducing what's real.
I'd placed my head under the table, under the armchairs
and under the bed, my feet up on the bookcases, on the
chairs and on the counters, with the camera right-side up
or upside down: in this way, in these curious positions, I
had begun to make this apartment, which had become
both strange and suffocating, my own again. It shifted
the spaces that enclosed me, produced images to refer
to, images to tuck away deep in my memory as if deep in
a drawer. I didn't much look at them, almost never, but
slowly they began to stand in for the real rooms, the real
walls of my apartment. It was only later, months later, that
words reappeared, not so much those of poems as those

of an essay for a project abruptly abandoned, chucked in

the bin, of which, today, I have no memory. The pictures, for their part, slept in my computer, forgotten for a few years. Coming back, then, years later, to the pictures I took while ill, was to realize that many of them are flat, technically weak, insignificant, banal, ugly. It was to resign myself to selecting the good ones and dismissing the bad ones, to sorting out what I experienced, to classifying images of my depression in accordance with aesthetic criteria. It was to force myself, also, to make new ones: to play the depressed person by reactivating the *interior wanderings*—technically, at first, then physically and, as the sessions wear on, more and more painfully. To attempt in vain to keep myself remote from the return of the illness I have never quite known myself to be rid of, because I am still, even now, suspicious of myself, of my insomnias, of my tremors, of my shallow breathing, my excesses, my feelings, my sensitiveness, always fearful of grief, disappointments, arguments, and betrayals, basically genuinely traumatized. Depression, when we come out of it, is quickly replaced by fear, with which it is obviously easier to live but which considerably impedes any push toward recovery, and these photographs have become, even sorted, even composed, the accumulated images of this fear that taints every bit of joy, every pleasure, every moment when I'm convinced I'm *sinking my teeth into life*. To attempt, then, to not fall back, but in sensing that it's coming, it's inevitable, that I'm playing with fire, to obstinately press on despite the fear, despite new insomnias, new tremors, despite the return—inevitable because of the pictures and, later, because of the words, of language, of poems—despite the return of a lighter version, less severe, less inconvenient, of the depression: a little melancholy, a little down, anxiety without excess. To come back to the pictures the illness produced, and then to create new ones and simultaneously write new poems (to make images with verbs, to metaphorize, reproduce the language of the ill person, to propel that language to the status of the poetic): to settle into a process that generates a new depression in which to (try not to) fall.

Daybreak already: the sun's brazen rays pierce the curtain and caress the walls as if they were soft. I catch their tenderness, día tras día, on full display, as my barely open eyes declare war on the world, starting with the concrete ceiling. *The battle will be a hard one*, I tell myself, *la lucha será*. La lucha is shipping out to the front lying down, muzzled, la garganta llena de polvo, throat full of tangling tongues, words on repeat, día tras día, like a square looming over the eyes, la garganta llena de yesterday's phrases, simple, incomplete, *the battle will be*. The rays reach me rough, overbearing. The ceiling, triumphant: every day, every morning, the world has me.

The bed is a square of concrete. Every day, I repeat: *I'd like it to become a ship, a raft, a rowboat; I'd like to navegar, acariciar the asphalt outside as if it were soft.* So my eyes draw circles on walls marked with an obscene light, *I'd like it if they disappeared.* I repeat the gaze's dance until dizzied, until the tormentas, temblores, terremotos y tsunamis come along, until horrified cries wreck the concrete and break up the perverse shimmers along the walls—the bed leaks, the ceiling heaves; the bed leaks, the ceiling heaves. Yo soy el horizonte, the open sea smushed between two plates. I spread out without moving, laid out vertically but not yet standing. Día tras día, cada madrugada, I'm set adrift. Castaway, out of bed.

TO COME BACK TO POEMS WRITTEN ON THE OTHER SIDE OF THE DEPRESSION—to ceaselessly rewrite them, shifting verb tenses, going from an *I* to a masculine *you*, then to a feminine *you*, dedicating them to a poet recently passed, Hélène Monette, then publishing them in a special issue of a literary magazine honouring her, amidst other poets writing on illness, bodies, choking, memory, grief. To then feel the fraud of it, of having doctored my writing, of having sold my illness for one more publishing credit, then coming to understand, later, that it was the anxiety speaking through me, the anxiety accusing me. So, to take the poems up again and clumsily set each below a picture produced while ill, selected with trembling hands and bated breath, picture hidden away for years in the depths of my computer as if a child curled up in a corner of their dwelling, a corner turned fortress or refuge, a house within a house, because *tout coin dans une maison, toute encoignure dans une chambre, tout espace réduit où l'on aime à se blottir, à se ramasser sur soi-même, est, pour l'imagination une solitude, c'est-à-dire le germe d'une chambre, le germe d'une maison.*[2] Then to tell myself I've got hold of something, that the depression I came out of years ago will—like exile, like memory, like love— take on new forms once more, will take to new dwellings as its own.

Gaston Bachelard
La poétique de l'espace

21

Hardwood, ceramic, linoleum, asphalt, suelo—mis pies, día tras día, seek material well-suited to receiving flesh charred by this unseemly sun penetrating las ventanas, desecrating surfaces: I exchange looks with the floor of the room como si fuera un extranjero. The ground gapes open to swallow mis palabras, the few remnants of a voice that still accompany my body. Slowly, I lie down on the ground, wait for a breach: the arm first, then the left shoulder and thigh, the legs and feet hold back my clamouring. Every day my head rests in agony.

The way I remember it, I'm in denial. I still haven't seen the doctor, I still haven't ever met with a therapist, I'm dragging a tiredness I chalk up to the Christmas holidays. My tremors, my insomnias, and my weight loss worry me in secret: last night, I looked up the symptoms of depression online.

The way I remember it, snow is coming down heavy and I like it, I think *rather reassuring, this snow*; I look for a bit of solace everywhere, even in the storm, even in the complaints of the brunch-eaters trickling in. The light in the restaurant is intense, as is the smell of fried egg and bacon that somehow doesn't quite work up my appetite. We're maybe twenty around the table, talking loudly, laughing, I'm unsure now if I laugh with the others, if I hear the jokes, if I talk, but I know that I don't eat much, that no one notices, that the mimosa hits me all at once. My best friend receives and eats ravenously; the way I remember it, I think *she's so pretty*, I also think *she sees none of it, she doesn't know me anymore*. I'm wrong; she'll be the one, during another outing a few days later, to get me talking about my listlessness, my night terrors, my sudden interest in death. She'll be the one to suggest getting out of the house one more time to see a doctor.

The way I remember it, my sister says *you're getting thinner*, I say, *yeah, I'm getting thinner*, we leave it at that. We make our way out of a successful brunch, and my sister will take a fond memory of it with her on her move to Europe. I don't remember it anymore.

TO COME BACK TO POEMS WRITTEN ON THE OTHER SIDE OF THE DEPRESSION— to express from far away, very far away, what was actually so close, as if an endless series of detours. I had previously written verse full of slashes and white spaces about what I thought of as my generation— in answer to a friend who wanted to include my poetry in his play. Very quickly, words, sounds, deconstructed, arrhythmic, and pseudoexperimental lines were rehearsed on stage by my friend, who is at ease with hybrid forms and departures in tone, himself engaged, long before I was, in a creative process favouring narratives involving a deconstructed, plural, political I. Reread, rewritten, published in magazines, and translated (flatly, much too literally) into Spanish to be read in public many times during a literary tour of Colombia, these poems were finally abandoned, having become unintelligible in the aftermath of so many detours: the words had lost their meaning, seemed worn away, gnawed down to the marrow. When, years later, I began writing new poems about depression, I felt the need to make my way to the window to look outside, beyond the apartment, beyond depression and time, to bind myself to something less solitary: those jarring thoughts that I'd once so quickly, almost automatically, set down on paper for my friend, written without thinking, didn't grapple with my generation, when it comes down to it, but with another community, that of those who spend hours staring out the window as if there were, on the other side, a long-lost past, loved ones and places long gone, a plural community that starts with my mother, with her gaze I so often replicated during my illness. My mother is the first one I see when I think of depression's inheritance, melancholy's legacy, my mother who herself has often suffered from depressions she could not name because of language, exile and solitude, because of her role as a Latina mother who has vowed to be strong, to hold on, to work too much: exiled mother, immigrant mother, Chilean woman, daughter of a mother also burdened by mental illnesses she also could not name because of poverty and the silences her family, her culture, and especially her religion imposed on her all her life. I remember my grandmother's fits, her manipulative episodes that would lead her to turn her Christian values, with extraordinary ease, on loved ones she wanted to punish, only to regret her actions with such force that she'd punish herself afterward with prayers and tears. I remember my own mother's prayers and tears, her melancholic glances, her glassy eyes, her ability to go from crying to laughing within a single utterance, all these moments where we laughed about this quality of my mother's that I shamefully recognized in myself, this quality we would blame on our culture of origin, and not without sexism: in Chile, I thought, women cry for two, as if men were unaware of the realm of emotions, as if they feared it with such impassioned hatred that they made it into horror stories to tell young boys—*emotions make you stupid*, children were told, and my father repeated this slogan to me when I cried after having been reprimanded (always emotional, I was a real crybaby as a child, like my mother I'd go from laughing to crying in no time, and I'd recognize in the disorderly, even exaggerated expression of my emotions a kind of strange escape from reality, a door to an ecstatic world made all the more alluring to me by snaps of *deja de llorar, las emociones te vuelven estúpido* forbidding my entry into it). For a time, I thought my father was inconsistent, contradictory, because he himself was driven by emotion when he spoke: it was the anger provoked by my tears that would at times make him snap *las emociones te vuelven estúpido*, but I quickly figured out that such fury was the only emotion permitted to men, whose firmness, stubbornness, implacability, and toughness—which they had to value over affection and tenderness—justified such enraged outbursts. In Chile, I pondered, women cry for two so that men, gorged with the anger deemed appropriate to their intelligence, might dominate them, discredit their suffering by reducing it to hysteria. It's what I believed, though I never believed my mother was hysterical but rather the product of a childhood nourished by this cultural sexism, by family wounds unknown to me, and by generations in the grip of social violence and mental illness, in short by a mixture sadly all too familiar in Latin America but also elsewhere, on other continents, in communities to which I belong and that do struggle against the reproduction of these kinds of violence. When it comes down to it, I

grew up in a Chilean family whose exile did not quite

rid it of its clichés, which is to say with a mother given to emotional excesses and a father that only gave in to those which matched the domineering role assigned to him. Indeed, my mother is the first person who comes to mind when I think of the inheritance of depression, but I also see Chile and its male chauvinism, I think of all the women who suffered from a hurt attributed to them to better disregard them, and I think of the men reduced to silence by the shame of hiding in the closet to cry; there are so many of us, bumping into each other at the crossroads of our miseries, assembled in this strange, unstable, intangible, and hopelessly quiet locale, and yet all of us itching to tell our stories broken open by grief and exile, a plural, diasporic space *that encompasses affect, emotion, and feeling, and that includes impulses, desires, and feelings that get historically constructed in a range of ways.* Ann Cvetkovich Depression: A Public Feeling To come back to these poems written on the other side of depression: a combative gesture to give shape, voice, and meaning to this space, to bring it out of the shadow, to free it from silence.

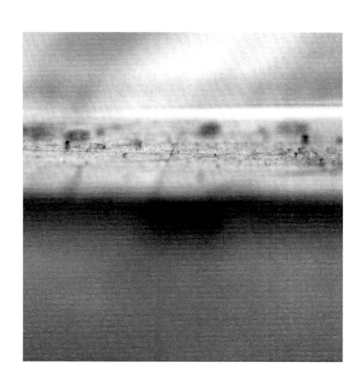

Every day, I trace roads across the parquet. The crawling wears my elbows down to the bone, the smell of animals huddled in the corners wears out my nose. Since all the floor's roads lead to the bed, every day my head ends up under the mattress. It's been a while since I've been scared of the monsters under there, I tame them with my daily wanderings just as *uno se aclimata al frío del invierno.* I greet them, I say *good morning.* Day after day, no reply. I tell them *one day I'll go outside.* I tell them *I'll go carve out some angels in the snow to watch the birds fly. Un día I'll rediscover the perfume of snowflakes, I'll let windblown powder tickle my nostrils.* I crawl, repeat my vows. I let the dust settle in my lungs, in the deceptive euphoria of a craving I can't stop.

I calculate the distance between the bedroom and the living room: my sprawled-out body doesn't make it to the couch. The ceiling, día tras día, is as obstinate as a cloud, it shows me the way. I get up quickly and hear my knees crack, feel my underwear tearing into my skin. I hear my eyes close as I waver. All I see are black and green splotches welling up in the deafening rhythm of my pulse; slowly, I lean into each beat of my heart. No me caigo, I say *no sé caer*. At the end of the hall: the TV's black screen and the dusty window. Between silence and racket, I sway. Trying to hear again.

The way I remember it, I wait four hours at the walk-in clinic. And yet I'm number 4, behind a very old woman who's kept a heavy silence, a mother with a green-looking child, and an agitated man who hasn't stopped coughing—at one point, the receptionist insists that he wear a face mask, which reassures me. The doctor jumbles up my name, starts off with my first family name, then my second given name before my first, and finally part of my second family name, then calls on two Latin American women. Amused by the coincidence, I wonder if these two other patients are suffering from the same ailment, if our state is the fruit of our lineage, of our exiles, of our forgotten languages, of our scattered families, until one of them, between coughing fits, says *este invierno me va a matar.* I surprise myself laughing, I tell myself *if I laugh, he won't believe me.*

The way I remember it, I'm consumed by fear of not being believed, fear that the doctor will peg me for a crybaby, a charlatan happy to waste his time for a bit of attention, for a bit of pity; I don't know if my illness is real or if I'm playacting, so I try to be convincing, I stop laughing and try to mimic the vacant look that has actually been

33

on my face for days. I tell him *I hope you'll believe me*, I say *I'm afraid I might be depressed*, I repeat *I don't know if you'll believe me.*

The way I remember it, he asks me why, and curtly asks me to tell my story. I'm caught off guard, I don't know if I'm expected to persuade him, I say *I'm not doing well*, and he starts over, his look shifts, he asks more precise questions, simpler ones, he warms up, listens like an adult trying to understand a story told by a child. I suddenly feel comfortable enough to turn my state into a narrative. The way I remember it, I tell him about my family's bursting apart, I list symptoms, I tell him about this test I took online. He laughs, which feels good, I tell myself *he believes me*, yet it saddens me. He sets down a questionnaire in front of me, asks me to fill it out while he sees other patients. As I read the awkwardly-phrased questions multiple times, I overhear a women speaking Spanish.

The way I remember it, I hear *gracias, doctor* before the doctor reappears, apologizes, I don't get why, I haven't noticed the time pass, the forty-five minutes spent just answering a questionnaire only seven questions long. He reads my answers, I think to myself *he's North African, his French is impeccable, he speaks Spanish, he looks at me with affection, he believes me: I'm lucky, I've been lucky in my unluckiness*, but I'm ashamed, I'm afraid of what he's about to say. He's taking too long to read my answers, I think about my master's thesis advisor in front of me reading poems I'd written, I think of my German language teacher by my side correcting my conjugations, I think of my father reading a warning from my fifth-grade teacher about homework I didn't do; I'm scared, I think about fear, I think about the silence that accompanies reading, I think about the silence that brings on fear, that stretches time and shrinks the room, I'm no longer breathing, increasingly short of breath, I'm losing myself, and suddenly there's nothing but emptiness, even the doctor's hands go blurry, my answers are no longer worth anything, I'm floating in another time, in another place, then he says *yes, you're suffering from depression.* He repeats it. He says *do you hear me?*

The way I remember it, he writes six prescriptions: *acupuncture, massage therapy, psychotherapy, vitamin D, omega 3, zopiclone.* I pick up the pile of papers without feeling, he says *you're trembling.* I look at my hands, I don't know what they're holding anymore. He says *get some sun, exercise, talk with your family, your friends. The receptionist will give you sick-leave papers. We'll try to get through this without antidepressants. Come back in a month. And… take care of yourself. I want to see you in a month.*

The way I remember it, I think *try to get through this without antidepressants* and I feel a bitter sort of joy when I replace *this* with *depression.* I think about the word, I hold it there, suspended in the air, taming it. It'll last months, nearly a year, this suspended word. I write it for the first time coming out of the doctor's, six hours after leaving home, in a message to a friend who sends back words of encouragement right away. I'll only see this friend again after my depression, once the word has become a story taking on endlessly renewed shapes.

Mirrors, windows, silvery trinkets: bouncing off each other, the living room's objects reflect and converse without a sound among the shadows. I say *I wish my gaze could shed light on them*, but instead I listen for what's being negotiated beyond the frames, in this perpetual offscreen where my body remains, mi cuerpo solitario que nadie ve. I squint; contrast the room with my thoughts, both distorted by my tears which, like this window kept shut, aren't giving way: one hand against the pane and the other on my face, I shape a new reflection.

The way I remember it, I wait an eternity in a terribly quiet hall that stands in for a waiting room at the downtown office of the therapist suggested and paid for by my employer. Only the whooshing of the air vents accompanies my breathing, which I'm trying in vain to keep under control, to slow down, but impatience always wins out over my attempts to meditate, so I look around for an image that might, if not calm me down, at least distract me: a single tattered magazine on the side table with a smiling woman in a bikini posing on the cover, and a lone, tiny, overexposed picture of the Rockies on the wall. I tell myself *looks like the Andes. Looks like the Alps... Looks like Mont Royal... Could be any fucking mountain.* I look at the woman in a bikini again, I wonder what I'm doing here.

The way I remember it, the therapist swings her office's green door open and gives me a tender look, she says *you're young I was expecting a grown man but you're young that's fun I'm sorry about the delay I have lots of work things to do keep piling up I'm sorry but come in sit down right there in the armchair sorry my office is a little messy lots of work lots of clients times are hard you understand so tell me what* 39 *brings you here it's not goin' so well eh not goin' so well oh wait I forgot I'll start the timer but don't worry it'll face me not you OK I'm starting the timer OK wait OK all good here we go we've got fifty minutes I know it says an hour on the sheet but it's actually fifty minutes fifty-five if we must it's so you don't bump into the next client you get it it's important you don't bump into each other it can be awkward imagine if you knew the next person and you come face to face might be awkward might be embarrassing you see that's why we have fifty minutes fifty-five if we must you follow good good good go right ahead what brings you here.* I open my mouth, she says *oh I forgot I'll be taking notes the whole way through I'll write lots you see I read my notes before each session or I don't remember my memory isn't super great and I have lots of clients so you see I'll be writing so I ask that you not talk too quickly and I might interrupt you but that's normal it's always like that go right ahead I'm listening to you I'm writing and I'm listening to you.* Her gaze and hand abruptly lock on to her pen and freeze. She's waiting for me to speak.

The way I remember it, I hesitate to speak for a long while, I look at her pen on the alarming stack of blank pages I suddenly feel bound to fill with details even if I run out of things to say, I don't know where to start, so I say *I'll start with* and she cuts me off, *the beginning let's start with the beginning go ahead.* I begin I'm not sure where and I speak slowly, and then a little more quickly, and I gradually find myself imitating the therapist's clip, the clip of her words at the beginning of our meeting, and I see her writing quickly while I'm talking, I see her struggling to keep up with me, *slow down a bit go on*, I see her motion to slow down with her left hand while the right one writes on at a furious pace, so I slow down a bit, just a little bit, all while watching the tip of her pen filling up page after page while I speak and I ask myself, as I'm talking, if my voice is leading the pen on or if it's the pen imposing this speed, I'm unsure now if I'm saying what the pen writes or if the pen is writing what I say, and I barely hear her fakely empathetic reactions, her few words uttered without a thought without letting her pen out of her sight as it keeps writing, I barely hear her *oh that's not nice*, her *oh yeah that's crazy*, and she repeats this phrase many times, so often that I ask myself, as I'm talking, if this is the phrase she's writing on her pages over and over again, *that's crazy, oh that's crazy*, and I think as I talk that a therapist shouldn't repeat this overused expression, *that's crazy*, because what I'm describing isn't crazy, I lived it, I'm living it, I'm not crazy, I'm not crazy but I'm slowly starting to feel, as I'm talking and as she's writing, that I'm going crazy, and right as I'm thinking, on the one hand, that she shouldn't say *that's crazy* and, on the other, that I'm going crazy, right then as a number of thoughts pile up in me as I keep talking, the therapist stops writing, blurts out *oh shit oh shit*, jumps up, leaves the room and slams the door.

The way I remember it, I stay quite still, immobilized by craziness. I haven't stopped staring at her pen, her pen now resting on the paper, stranded atop the words she left behind in this terribly quiet office of hers. Only whooshing of the air vents accompanies my breathing, and the ticking of the timer she didn't turn off when she ran out. The way I remember it, I think about the smiling woman in a bikini because I still wonder what I'm doing here.

The way I remember it, the therapist comes back with the same tender look, *I apologize I'm sorry I had an appointment for something else another thing a parcel a package a person who had to get something to me it doesn't concern you but there you go I had forgotten it but now it's all good I hope she isn't mad it's someone from another office in the building it's a long story just a something unexpected I forgot about you see you've got to keep the peace with the neighbours you see but don't worry I'm listening I remember everything I'm listening and*—she looks at her timer—*we've only got a few minutes left so could you please wrap up.*

The way I remember it, I don't wrap up, I say *well that's it.* I no longer know what came next, I only remember having glanced at the Rockies on the wall on my way out.

Yesterday, a tornado reduced a city to nothing at all. I know it because on TV the debris formed a forest ready to welcome new bodies, new woods, new waters, a bit of tar to pour on the agony of the survivors: the silence of a man still harmonizes, día tras día, with the prayer of a woman whose pain puffs her eyes. I know it because the flat and vast forest on TV was somehow getting denser, glutting itself day after day on a half-full mess. On the screen: llantos, rezos, gritos, airwaves I now send to the living room, envying the history that didn't set me down there, in the eye of the tornado, envying the destiny of the sobrevivientes, heroes on TV, heroes of uprooted trees amidst the winds and animals passing by so very calmly, tenderly como caricias que no consigo because the rubble fills the TV screen, smothers my voice in this tormenta failing day after day to break the living room's unbearable stillness.

TO COME BACK TO POEMS WRITTEN ON THE OTHER SIDE OF THE DEPRESSION—to the solitude from before, and finding myself, ironically, alone again to keep on healing. *For me the real healers were seclusion and time*, the seclusion of the writer, the time of writing, or rather of rewriting: at the heart of these now well-worn poems, I set a bomb like the one I've so often wanted to drop in my apartment, just as I wanted to do on language itself, on the narration or story that was unfolding, but also on my own French because this tongue of mine that isn't my mother tongue, this language I write, think, teach, this language is the one that failed me during my illness, became the language of the other, became foreign again (had it ever even stopped?). Only a babbling, stuttering kind of speech remained, an unrecognizable thing clinging to my skin, a foreign body on my own body, *belle façade taillée dans une « langue étrangère »*.[3] My mother-tongue Spanish, for its part, was still there, still just as incomplete, instinctive, and awkward as ever, still just as connected to my very emotional mother, so prone to flight and melancholy, and pledged as I am to nostalgia. I remember naming things in Spanish as if to remind myself this other language wasn't other, that it could be mine as French was before it started playing tricks on me, before it drifted away: horizon, horizonte; window, ventana. To

William Styron
Darkness Visible: A Memoir of Madness

Kristeva

look at the horizon out the window in Spanish, mirar el horizonte a la ventana to see my mother's face out there, to hear amidst her tears a few songs and nursery rhymes like melancholic hymns in tribute to the depressed, the lost, the suicides, to those whose suffocating melancholy forces them to stare at a window for help they can't quite name. (My bilingualism is riches to me, not only because I can express myself in two languages but because I can make liberal use of them: one can deconstruct the other, one can save me when the other stumbles—so, which is the language of my melancholy? The French that failed me? The mother-tongue Spanish that made its way back, not unpainfully, to awkwardly identify what suddenly no longer had a name?) To come back to the poems written on the other side of the depression was to come to really understand, by doubling back, that writing and languages have been part of the healing process: in seclusion and in time, it's writing y los idiomas that bound me to others, from an *I* to a *we*, from a *yo* to a *nosotrxs*, from myself to a community anxious to name the hurt.

Arranged before me, slices and slices repletas de palabras, títulos y nombres, llenas de códigos y colores, according to an order that concealed itself as it kept going: tal vez es mi memoria which, crossed out, cross-hatched, scratched off, wastes its time and returns incessantly to the same objects firmly stuck in the present, the implacable, unalterable present surrounding these slices of books with an aura of the here-and-now, with a thick outline like a shelf without perspective, history, or depth, with a border along fronteras that blank out sentences and no longer contain anything but ditches, dribbles, smears. No hay más palabras, there are no more titles. Simple surfaces: these slices remain slices, these books remain images.

The way I remember it, I've stopped reading, but I spend an awful lot of time unemotionally looking at my books without really grasping their contents, as if they've become hollow things, emptied of their words, simple sheets, papers, pigments, dots, abstract lines in space, and yet that day, fooled by the regular and precarious resurgence of an energy that always wanes just when I most believe in my deliverance, right when I'm convinced that I'm out of the woods, safe, saved from the world and myself, fooled by this energy that disappears exactly when I think I'm healed, just then, I decide to brave the winter cold, particularly arduous this year because of the many polar vortexes, to go pick up extra books, raring to read essays, studies, and dissertations on mental health that connect questions, among others, of race, sexual diversity, and grief, and more specifically writings on the affective turn particular to queer studies, so that I may think about depression in circumstances of immigration and queerness, with the aim of one day writing a book on my condition. High on this notion of new research, new readings, new epistemologies to explore as if suddenly intrigued by a country that must be visited to learn the language, I brave the polar cold with tenacity and unrivalled ease: I walk twenty minutes through Montreal's empty streets on my way to the local library, just as empty, and then I notice that I'm trembling, that I no longer feel my feet, that my ears are red and overheating because of the radical temperature shift, that my shoulders won't quite relax. So, I take the time, as I enter the library, to feel my body unscrunch, react to the excessive heating that violently cuts through the arctic air, I go quite still to better feel the blood find its way back to my fingers, my feet, my ears, and feel the swift melting of the tiny icicles between my eyelashes, I think *feels like I've been crying*, I think *is this how meditating feels?*

The way I remember it, this brief meditation gives me a rather serene, floaty air, and I press confidently onward through the library stacks with a sure-footed rhythm, as if in a familiar place, in a school long attended, in my neighbourhood, on my own street, in the long hallway at my best friend's place, she has me over all the time, and I sway my hips, I've got a pop song in my head and I sway my hips like I'm on a catwalk, I stop right in front of a shelf, I find the book and I repeat the dance four or five times, in different stacks for different books I set on a table to the same beat so as to peruse them, the same song in my head handily guiding me, the chair under my thighs, my elbows on the table, the pages between my fingers, my eyes on the beginning of a word, then another, then another, then a diagonal line all the way down to the last word on the page, the next one a bit jittery, I think *nothing to worry about*, I keep going, and the next one won't keep still, my hands start shaking, the books give way like the words on the pages, like the letters that calmly jumble together, like the floor that sinks and the stacks that start to spin. The way I remember it, I felt that I was confronting the world via the cold I endure and the books I read, but the world is trickier than that, the world reminds me yet again that the weakness that's stricken me feeds on these shows of strength that end as suddenly as they begin.

The way I remember it, the rhythm that had energized me abruptly abandons me, yields to a yawning silence, and it's this abandonment that keeps me there, unmoving, sitting in front of a pile of books transformed into elusive objects emptied of their promise of new knowledge, symbols of my accumulated incapacities that I contemplate, numbly, for long minutes, maybe hours, as I do daily at home, in front of my own books, in front of my own library that no longer reminds me of anything, no past readings, no memories, no outings, and this expedition, this getting out of the house, becomes another failure.

The way I remember it, I spend the following hours battling the cold now nestled inside me, drinking tea and coffee by my frosty window, I tell myself *all those books left on the library table*, I tell myself *someday I'll have to actually write this book of mine*, and I keep drinking tea and coffee, patiently staring at the window. The way I remember it, I don't know if I'm waiting to be healed or fooled again, maybe I'm just waiting to no longer feel cold.

TO WRITE NEW POEMS—to attempt to reproduce the
ear-splitting language that wailed inside me, and to end
in failure: this language doesn't exist. It's but scattered
and limp reflections made up of obvious enumerations—
hurt, pain, death—and a few short phrases—*my back
hurts, I'm afraid of…* What follows are spirals, never-
ending loops built on thoughts that give rise to nothing
but themselves— *à force d'enchaînements, se rétrécit pour
bientôt se refermer une boucle morbide que résume l'absurde
tautologie : je souffre puisque je suis en train de souffrir…*[4]
Writing poems is not meant to reproduce thinking, even
as ailing, as rhythmic (the language of the depressed
person is so alien, so uneven, constantly swinging
between full and empty, between talkative periods and
huge silences, that it carries an extraordinary rhythm
which I've often, during my illness, wanted to reproduce
in writing, but since I was no longer managing to write—
as if, between the screen and me, between the paper and
me, was a creature sucking all of my knowledge, all of my
intelligence, the whole of my ability to express myself—
since I was no longer managing to write, I found myself
confined to what I had written at another time and
which I couldn't read, to what I was thinking but could
not get out, since *mes anciens alliés, ces milliers de mots que
j'avais éperdument assemblés, étaient devenus ma prison : la*

Céline Curiol
*Un quinze
août à Paris:
Histoire d'une
dépression*

rigidité de mes déductions dressait des paravents tout autour
de moi;[5] I was thus reduced to an even more depressing
silence that plunged me deeper into self-pity and left
me even more entangled in the never-ending loop of
suffering because of suffering). Isn't writing really meant
to endow thoughts with languages, forms, new and above
all excessively various meanings? To get out of these
loops, everything is worth a try, to break free of painful
thoughts and silences, of the cages we build ourselves,
everything is fair game. Everything: photography, poetry,
and now (maybe even more than photography and
poetry) the personal story and essay. Writing new poems,
then, and returning to the old hurt as if making peace
with an enemy: be wary, keep your guard up, expect a
new rift, plan for the worst. The hurt comes back fast, first
with spiralling thoughts, with loops seemingly leading to
madness, to panic, which then give way to such marred
sleep you cease to distinguish the dreamed from the real Clément Rosset
because *la boucle tend à se boucler, ou les deux extrémités du* *Route de nuit:*
Épisodes cliniques
tunnel à se rejoindre, les cauchemars du jour – de certains
jours – venant rendre visite à ceux de la nuit.[6] But I keep
a certain distance; I stay alert to the effects of the loop
while knowing I won't be able to avoid it: realizing that
all the periods—of depression, of healing, of creating—
are part of a process as never-ending as exile, as memory,
as love. Getting through to the other side of a depression
is to grant it, despite yourself, an everlasting place in your
life, a place that produces new processes, that induces new
loops: I was depressed and thus incapable of creating,
then I healed and so was able to create, and now I'm

creating something about depression, which takes me back to that initial state, and has me recognize in myself now the symptoms from back then; am I going to lose my creativity again?

I say *the living room, speechless*: my words without an echo. The living room, speechless, between three walls and a window, encloses monotonous images I'm suddenly taking in as if they were new. My head settles between a wall and another one, my body straight as a tripod in front of a picture frame, then the tripod wobbles because the reflections loop around me: within the frame, other frames, and despite my voice, my face on repeat. *The living room, speechless*; my words without an echo. But this time my body answers: I fall on my side, balled up, hands creased, wrinkled, gone see-through from grasping nothing, touching nothing; these newborn hands could gouge my eyes out. I curl in on myself on the cold, dry floor, take the shape of elderly feet that have done too much walking, or those of prisoners going in circles between three walls and a set of bars, murmuring the same phrases until they've lost all meaning, making loops in space, loops in time. I say *sala de estar*, I translate *living room, room to be in*, and I rise; I take in the frame one more time.

The living room, I say, room of books and glass, sala abierta al mundo, and empty room. Día tras día, appalled, I fear its panes and comforts. *The living room*, I repeat, guerrero. I make my way to it crawling, first on my stomach, then on my back. If at least the parquet became water, the ceiling a sky, I could drift along, pero mi maldita cabeza bangs into the TV. *I'd like it*, I repeat, *if the living room caved in on me*. Nothing moves, nothing collapses, ni siquiera mi cráneo now smushed against the screen. The living room: a cruel stillness, its light spread over its unoccupied surfaces, its ceremonial bibles, its reflections and images, its chassis, statues and gravestones. The living room, waiting room, remainder. Nocturno, día tras día, this is where I give up: the sala de estar empties my head and covers it in dust.

TO WRITE NEW POEMS—to write new poems (to suddenly find a new tautology). Which is to say, no, I'm not losing my creativity. It's true that I've come back to the drift, the anxiety, the trouble sleeping, the hypersensitivity, the hypochondria, and the anorexia I struggled with during my depression—had any of them really left me? While healing, during this buffer period wherein I wrote, photographed, travelled, studied, taught, didn't they all stay with me, these symptoms nestled deep inside my being now strong enough to hold them off, to deny them, to make sure they stay dormant till this inevitable creative project wakes them up? Yet I see these symptoms coming from far off with such a lightness and faintness that they seem harmless; so I can play with them, take them up as tools that don't really wipe out the danger and fear of lapsing back into depression but also don't spoil my capacity to sit down and write, to take pictures, to read. My thoughts are marred by these symptoms, sure, but to the benefit of the language I seek to (re)produce, the one that places us *au sein de la voix*,[7] the one that talks too much and seemingly says nothing, the one that grows denser as it repeats itself, forgetting—as the verbiage heaps on—to produce a meaning that might heal the ailing person of all their pains, a language that risks falling flat, exhausted, breathless, lifeless, to completely

Kristeva

59

give way to a noxious silence, to a dull ominous air, herald
of the end, of a death we don't know how to avoid any
other way than by picking these same words back up,
after a night of nightmares and insomnia, these words
that lead, and yet we know it well, to the silence that
leads to the night that leads to the words that lead...
How can we not, then, yearn for death? Thanks to these
symptoms that have returned to me like enemies with
whom, because they're enemies, I maintain my distance
and prudence, I manage to write this language down,
to say it, to express it, to give it a shape that propels it,
along with the death it yearns for, out of me. To write
new poems in order to place the melancholy and its
deadly loops outside of me, to settle within a chosen loop
where the shapes of its enunciations are plural, shifting,

Cvetkovich
Depression: A
Public Feeling

and performative: *Ideally, I'd like those forms of testimony
to offer some clues about how to survive those conditions
and even to change them, but I'd also settle for a compelling
description, one that doesn't reduce lived experience to a list
of symptoms and one that provides a forum for feelings that,
despite a widespread therapeutic culture, still haven't gone
public enough. It's a task that calls for performative writing.*
I wondered, then, how this project might end, if such
a looping, spiralling, performative writing were even
likely to have an end, if healing would be part of it, if
there ought to be a happy ending. Foolish question: no
happy endings with depression. At best, we come back
from it forever living with its ghosts, vestiges and relics;
at worst... The only happy ending is that of mediation:

if readers hold these poems in their hands it's that death

hasn't come yet, it's that the opposite of death came along, it's that there was a battle, another one, this time against the return of the depression I myself recalled, remade, reperformed, and which brought about pictures, poems, essays, personal stories—all kinds of shapes mediation can take. Maybe mediation is the only way to avoid lapsing back into depression? Instead of turning away and fighting off depression's eventual return (that is, by avoiding all stressful, anxious-making situations, authoritarian and domineering people, challenges and lessons—might as well die!), draw depression back to you, call on it like you might invoke an evil spirit to exorcize, in spectacular fashion, the person it possesses. Attempt imprudence, play with fire to better control it, to battle it one more time, so that this battle brings about a language, various shapes that, instead of putting an end to the battles, evoke victory.

The way I remember it, this time I have an appointment
to see my doctor for my monthly check-up to determine if
my sick leave should continue or stop, an anxious-making
exercise among many anxious-making exercises I have
had to subject myself to without exception for months,
from the moment my first appointment consigned me
to a system where, despite my being its principal subject,
I'm seemingly just an instrument, the object carried from
place to place, from one appointment to the other, from
one outing to the next. During these monthly check-
ups I fill out the initial questionnaire again to evaluate
the seriousness of my state, the same seven awkwardly
phrased questions that feel so complicated to answer;
instead of simply saying I feel this or that, I think this
or that, I want this or that, it demands that I answer
the questions in terms of frequency: *as long as I can
remember / at least two weeks / one week / a few days /
never; or, occasionally, almost every day / over seven days
/ several days / never.* So for each question I ask myself
if the frequency is calculated from the last appointment
or from the initial onset of the symptoms, I don't know
what to do with the states that don't last, the ones that
come and go sporadically, like fear, anger, or paranoia, I

don't know what to do with the states the questionnaire doesn't address, like hypochondria and distrust, above all I don't know what to do with the intensity of these states, the stubbornness with which my taste for life remains lost to me or the exaggerated intensity of the despair I feel, and then I remember that, moving forward, I was going to consider the first of these questionnaires as the starting point, like the very first document in a long series of documents to fill out to regulate my depression: prescriptions to get to my pharmacists, receipts to keep in a safe place in case of an audit, letters to hand over to the college's human resources department, invoices and forms to provide to my insurer to signal the continuation of the oxymorons materialized by the terms *sick leave* and *leave of absence*; so many rhetorical contortions at play with these emptied-out words constrained to boxes, smothered by these stamped, signed, dated, folded papers carefully tucked away in an envelope, shuffled about so that we may, when it comes down to it, make use of them in ways that escape me because, right now, I can't read, write, teach, think, communicate, speak.

Indeed, the way I remember it, I barely talk anymore, each sound that comes out of my mouth is an extra pain, particularly the *h*'s and *r*'s. I'm convinced I'm suffering from tonsillitis, it reappears in times of crisis ever since I was a kid, and this time the crisis is never-ending. In reality, each doctor's appointment comes with its own new ailment: last month it was my head, the month before that a plugged ear, next month it'll without a doubt be worrying chest tightness, this month it's tonsillitis, but the doctor, annoyed and expeditious, hastily examines me and says *no, only redness, stop smoking.* I insist, he says *it's in your head* as he tosses a few things in the bin full of wooden sticks. I receive his words like a punch to the throat, I say nothing else, I maintain this silence I've slowly gotten used to, a shameful, hurt, humiliated silence, and then he stops, takes a breath, and tells me *I'm going to prescribe an antibiotic for your throat, take it if, and only if, it still hurts in three days.* I smile as he fills out this piece of paper he'll add to the documents I'll take with me when I leave this place, these papers I suddenly think of as my deliverance, because thanks to him, thanks to this paper full of scribbles I'll hand to the pharmacist in exchange for pills I'll undoubtedly never swallow, I now have permission to spend the next three days tending to my tonsillitis instead of my depression.

I name each piece of furniture, I say *mesa, comptoir, silla,* then the words bang into each other, bounce off and shatter, break off into other words, lick other tongues, make up paths I take blindly only to knock into other walls, only to sink into the limits of dead ends. I repeat las palabras that carve out stoplines in the air, in short, crisscrossing cuts. Between la mesa y yo, between the counter and me, between the silla y yo, impasses map themselves out. The things I name stop time, constantly give rise, every day, to arrhythmias and ricochets, arrhythmias and ricochets, echoes and facades, arrhythmias, blanks. Of clashes and rackets, of these chattering moments, día tras día I give in to a deadly quiet, as they say, I give in to a body frozen in front of parts of palabras laid bare at the centre of a kitchen-city where ya nada se dice, where nothing ricochets anymore, where nothing's in the works as if it's a museum hopelessly blank. In total stillness, in a speechless contemplation of everything walling this in, I wait for an image to come. I wait for the next din to come along.

TO READ ESSAYS ABOUT DEPRESSION—first, to seek them out frantically while I'm supposed to be working on another project, a novel tackling memory and exile but also melancholy, grief, and suicide. And then fly off to a sunny, festive city with bleakly titled books under my arm. Barcelona, city of love, had never seen me in such a pitiful state. I spent weeks reading accounts of sadness, misfortunes, and thoughts of death that eventually got the best of me: quickly, I was forced to accept that my researcher's remove was shrinking before my eyes and bringing me back, despite the joys of Barcelona, to a wintry past, to my cold Montreal apartment surrounded by churches and construction sites. Accepting the return of my depression while I was away, in my favourite city in Europe, didn't, however, stop me reading. On the contrary, the more I suffered (headaches, backaches, chest pains, sprains, tonsillitis, insomnia, etc.) the more I read, and maybe I read so much just because these bodily pains, considered separate from the illness, don't in and of themselves call to mind the clinical term, now subject to such common usage, and not without controversy: Depression is *too blank and unhelpful a term to explain what I was living, and the catch-all term* anxiety *that I often use here is also a vague and feeble substitute. The sprained ankle, however partial and tangential to the*

Cvetkovich
Depression: A Public Feeling

69

real problem, tells the story. Not unlike Cvetkovich's ankle sprain, my pains were identifiable, and by tangibly associating them with specific body parts, I paradoxically instigated the process of distancing my pains from my depression and, because of this distance, I took up a rather damning perspective on my situation, which in reality is that of a truly privileged person; it was with shame and a certain contempt that I recognized these pains and tears that made me want to read inside a sunny

Eve Kosofsky
Sedgwick
*A Dialogue
on Love*

Barcelona: *I expect there are tears here. Not copious tears, but seeping ones: I think of them contemptuously as the tears of privilege.* Pain, craving, and contempt reiterated: these simultaneous feelings initiated the process of making a narrative out of my experience that began with the need to read; from then on I felt an energy akin to joy but subdued, shaky, obsessive, frightening, energy that takes hold of a researcher who knows he's found something but doesn't know where it'll lead, something that opens an exhilarating breach but prolongs the work ahead, something that throws you off-kilter and blinds you to the world's beauty—beaches, bodies, lights at night. To read despite Barcelona and despite the hurt, because to read about the hurt is to place it at an appropriate distance to better understand it, perceive it, feel it, live it. It was inevitable: if I read about the hurt, obviously I'd write about it; no doubt it's what pushed me to read so many essays on depression. I couldn't resist the insatiable craving for at times complicated, at times clinical, often sensitive, always thoughtful recounted. I even dared to

believe this mounting anxiety was the thing making me

so hungry for all of it: in addition to preventing me from truly tasting the pleasures of Barcelona, it did, yes, push me to read more, as if my craving was endless, aware though I was that these readings were in turn feeding my anxiety—a new loop, though this time driven by a clearer, even more vital hunger. *Intellectual curiosity about one's own illness is certainly born of a desire for mastery. If I couldn't cure myself, perhaps I could at least begin to understand myself.* To get there, I felt I first had to understand where others were coming from: I was desperate to know why Siri Hustvedt would suddenly start shaking when giving speeches, why William Styron's success wasn't enough to lessen his death wish, why surviving breast cancer plunged Eve Kosofsky Sedgwick into a deep depression. I needed others to thoughtfully, but also unflinchingly, tell me their own story and attempt to explain it with science, philosophy, history, sociology, and literature— every discipline that could, from afar or close up, help us make this illness less enigmatic, maybe even less painful, especially more political. *Help us*: suddenly I understood this kind of phrase was why I had been reading so much. To make a we take shape. *We*, not only my mother's face. *We*, these melancholy people. *We*, who have made it to the other side of this hurt without, thank God, losing ourselves to it. We, nosotros, nosotras: somos sobrevivientes.

Siri Hustvedt
The Shaking Woman or A History of My Nerves

TO READ ESSAYS ABOUT DEPRESSION—to encounter a myriad of ideas, seductive turns of phrase, and spectacular formulations capping off occasionally abstract reflections—the essay, like poetry, has this thing for falling. We so often take a tumble while reading an essay, while reading a poem, while writing them, also. We fall with the words, then get back up with the next paragraph, the next poem, hardly but courageously, so that a new ecstasy is produced and makes us fall once again. One after the other, one atop the other, such reflections can nonetheless produce an undesirable effect. I recall the moment when, sitting on a patio, I was reading the crucial chapter of *Tomber sept fois, se relever huit* (literally *Fall Seven Times, Get Back Up Eight*) wherein Philippe Labro, confined to his kitchen, torn between the knife and the rope, yearns for death, then finds his way back by thinking about his children only to notice that this simple scene which felt like an eternity and ended with his acknowledgement, finally, of the gravity of his depressive state in fact only lasted a minute, which forces him to ask himself a fundamental question about the relationship to time imposed by depression: *C'est quoi, le temps réel ? Donnez-moi une définition, s'il vous plaît.*[8] I recall this reading which selfishly revealed my own unease about places and time to me. I could

Philippe Labro
*Tomber sept fois,
se relever huit*

73

hear a kid playing, a boy calling for his friend, a woman arguing on the phone; I believed these books had the potential to wall me in, to separate me from Barcelonian life vividly unfolding in front of me, outside of me. I was at my most hurt by my new hurt: I was beginning to feel disgusted by this city and eager to get back to Montreal, but then I simultaneously felt disgust for Montreal, an inconsolable sadness for the impossibility of staying in Barcelona forever, and contempt for myself for failing to appreciate its true value. I was looking for culprits: the books? This hurt come back from the past? This pain that, without my knowing, crossed the ocean with me to track me down again, like an enemy, in my favourite city? Yes, it was the culprit, this hurt reappeared post-healing to isolate me anew: Barcelona's full-throated exclamations could do nothing about it. The essays I was reading then seemed devoid of meaning, harebrained, whiny. *I*

Hustvedt *confess that in my gloomier moments I have wondered if a whole host of intellectual theories don't fall into the category of grand confabulations.* In the same breath, I took note of an obvious fact: Barcelona had no use for me, for my presence; I was just another tourist, a privileged tourist with the means to travel, with a good handle on Spanish but who doesn't speak a word of Catalan, a tourist who, despite his isolation and his silence, despite his readings and his hurt, remained part of this mass of invaders I intensely wished to dissociate myself from, and so life in Barcelona, apart from my mood and state of mind, carried on—whether I heard it or not, whether I lived it

74 or not. Trying was pointless: I'd always be a stranger. My

community wasn't there. It was elsewhere. In addition to arranging the old hurt within a coherent methodology, language, and discourse, in reality, these books made up my community: by reading, by playing with the distance and closeness to the experience of depression these readings provoked, I was suddenly less alone. *Reading,* *after all, is a way of living inside another person's words.* No, I wasn't walled in: with all the expressions, formulations, verbal tics, and thoughts of these depressed people I read, I was building a new house in Barcelona, transforming the cage into a home the walls of which would, from then on, be those of other people's depression. Quietly, as my readings went on, I was better able to see the colours, to pick up on nuances and textures, to breathe in the fragrances and converse, in good conscience, with this illness that, without leaving me be, no longer burdened me: time and solitude saved me again, sure, but this time it was also Barcelona, and the words of others I inhabited.

The way I remember it, it's a short walk to this new therapist's office, which is actually in his apartment, Wolfe Street, a couple of doors down from Cabaret Mado, closed at this early morning hour; I walk past it and think about the drag queens that come through it each evening, and about the young ones by their sides like little fish among the sharks, about the gangs of boys I never belonged to, who laugh with the queens, who scream with the queens, who make videos and take selfies with the queens, who pick on the weaker ones and worship the strongest among them. *From now on*, I tell myself, *Cabaret Mado...* I don't make it to the end of my sentence, but the effect is the same: from now on this place's colours no longer celebrate anything.

The way I remember it, this phrase, *from now on*, I'll repeat it like a hook.

The way I remember it, the window lets in too little light to properly make out the space, I guess at the contours of the brown walls and old pieces of furniture, mostly I see cigarette smoke wafting about the bookshelves. I think *smells like a sweaty bar*, and just then I hear a nasally voice call after me as if I were a child or dog: *come, come. At the back of the apartment. Go through the doors in front of you. I'm in the office, past the living room, past the kitchen. Go through all the doors all the way back. Come.* I open a door that leads to the living room and fabric brushes my arm, a heavy, sparkling fabric, a dress hanging off the wall, a summer dress, black and purple, covered in sequins, synthetic fur along the cleavage, I think *a drag queen's dress* and I trip on a feather boa.

The way I remember it, another door, not as heavy, not as thick, leads to a kitchen overflowing with empty beer bottles, then yet another door to a room packed with colourful, brightly patterned sheets; bits of rug and fabric hang on the office's walls, along with necklaces and pictures of celebrities: Céline Dion, Dalida, Édith Piaf, Marilyn Monroe, Barbara, Michèle Richard. I think of the Rockies and the woman in a bikini at the other therapist's office downtown. The way I remember it, an enormous cat is loafing on the couch that's supposed to be for me: *get off, Chagrin. Company gets to sit. You can pick him up, he's lazy but harmless.* I nudge the cat with the back of my hand, I think of the allergies I'll soon be suffering, and I sit on the hair left behind by Chagrin, in front of the therapist who looks me over and smiles with this look I sometimes get when I walk by Mado's, when I cross paths with older men that look me up and down with a sneer like an invitation they can't quite put into words for fear of refusal, of rejection, of the scandal they might cause; maybe these looks and smiles are actually more like supplications, attempts to wordlessly say *I'm begging you tell me you want me*, and maybe these men no longer know what to do among the gaggles of boys who hang around the drag queens like little fish among the sharks, maybe they can no longer tell what they can or can't say, what they can or can't look at, if they really can or can't try their hand at a night of romance and risk yet another rejection that, despite its daily occurrence, will never cease to be painful, so I tell myself that this therapist checking me out, looking me over like I'm one of the neighbourhood boys, he might be one of them himself, once young and popular, now old and quiet, and everything in here, the dress, the boa, the beers, Chagrin rubbing up against my leg and Michèle Richard's eternal wink, are the remnants of a bygone time when people made love, when the nights were hot, and I think *our scene is cruel*, and my look softens despite the lewdness of his tone as he says *now then, tell me what's wrong.*

The way I remember it, he speaks slowly, he rolls his *r*'s and stretches out the first words of his sentences to lend them more of a saccharine quality. Something about his voice repulses me, something about his lilt, about the way he sets his lips as if to give his words a running start, about how he squints so that I may better understand he's trying to look beyond me, about the fleeting caresses he gives the little cards he holds atop his crossed legs, about the circular motion his foot repeats above the carpet, about Chagrin's purring. I say *I'm allergic to cats, can he leave the room?* The way I remember it, he covers Chagrin in kisses before he shoos him out, calls him *my big boy* or *my big kitty* or *my big teddy bear*, no matter, he says it with an obscene tone, I look away, but my gaze lands on Michèle Richard once more. He says *I'll be taking notes on my little cards, and I'll hand them over at the end with a few encouraging phrases for the harder times.* Words he says with the same tone he used to say *my big boy my big kitty my teddy bear*, the same tone he uses to say *well then, my dear, tell me, tell me.*

The way I remember it, the session proceeds without major incident: his look remains the same as I tell my story, his lips never tighten, he never ceases to check me out, to sneak furtive glances at my chest, my hands, my feet, my leg which, earlier, Chagrin was rubbing up against. Occasionally, he writes a few words on a card he then slowly places between his legs, sometimes interrupts me to read its content: *I hear my anger but am I hearing it out? / Don't expect the worst and the best will come to be, don't expect the best and disappointment will flee. / Cry your rage and rage your anger.* The way I remember it, I don't react, these phrases make no sense to me, I don't know what that means, rage your anger, cry your rage, I change the subject, I bring up my Chilean roots, I talk about exile, whereupon he writes nothing on his cards but flashes a glinting smile, he says *hablas español*, I answer *yes I speak Spanish*, he keeps smiling, he says *yo también, un poquito*. I don't respond, I think of these men outside Mado's who look me up and down because of the colour of my skin, these men who sometimes invite me home with them in an atrocious Spanish to which I never know what to respond because I'm caught off-guard amidst so much solitude and hopelessness, amidst so much tactlessness and ignorance, amidst so much desire and abandon, amidst so much candor and confidence; I'm speechless, I want to change the subject again, but I'm out of anecdotes, already I'm at the end of my story, I'd rather know his.

The way I remember it, he tells me about the Dominican Republic, about that Island music and those young Latinos *who really know how to move*, he asks me if I'm gay, he asks me if I have a boyfriend, if my boyfriend is Latino, I say *no, he's white*, no reaction, he tells me I should really see the Islands, under the sun, down in the Dominican Republic or someplace else, anywhere in the Caribbean, I start to run with it, I say *Cuba*, he says *why not, yes, Cuba*, I say *Haiti*, he says *I don't know, Haiti's a bit sad, no?* I say it's the Caribbean, he says *that's true, but...* he stops a moment to write something on a little card he sets down between his legs, *down there in the Dominican Republic, the people are happy, um, people... what's the word, um, people... fil... felix? Feliz, feliz people. Buena gente.* He has no idea how to pronounce the g, I correct him with as much arrogance as I can possibly muster, with all the fury I can scrounge up inside myself, a fury I draw straight from contemporary forms of colonialism: *gente, one says gente, gggggente*, I think *maybe this is it, raging your anger.* I think *crying should come next.*

The way I remember it, he makes a pompous display of presenting me with the little cards: *you're a bright young man, a lovely man, you know yourself well, you don't need me. Read these little cards when things get rough, you'll be fine. But my door is always open, whenever you like. I'm here for you.* He repeats *I'm here for you.* His empathy—so simple, inappropriate, too intimate—nevertheless manages to move me.

The way I remember it, the final card features a little sun beside two simple words: *Dominican Republic.*

TO READ ESSAYS ABOUT DEPRESSION—and to then feel genuine discomfort that has nothing to do with the illness but modulates it, adorns it in colours that reduce me to silence, an intense yet so very familiar uneasiness. *Regardless of their gender or place of origins, these writers did have one thing in common: they were white. All of them. Which placed me in the peculiar position of having very little choice but to look to these white people for some sense of validation, some basic understanding of who I am as a depressive and, ultimately, as a person underneath this illness.* I'm used to being in the minority in most of the cultural spaces I'm active in: Quebec's literary, artistic, academic and pedagogical spaces. My communities are relatively homogenous and I often take up a funny role in them—though I'm sometimes labelled a killjoy or radical, mostly I'm told my racialized perspective is a necessary one, and most of the time I'm listened to, what I say is heard, an attempt, for better or worse, is made to understand the difference, because, among other things, my studies, my diplomas, my work, and my bylines have legitimized my place in these spaces mostly populated by people who benefit from many privileges—especially in relation to class. It is said that depression is a rich person's illness; it's obviously not that simple, and melancholy isn't strictly a white condition either. Nevertheless, we have to turn to

Meri Nana-Ama Danquah "Writing the Wrongs of Identity"

fiction to see depression, madness, isolation, silence, and the unmooring and suffering of the mind acknowledged, thanks to the works of non-white people, many of them from modest backgrounds, situated within heavily stratified social systems made up of various repressions (racial and colonial above all) and power imbalances— think of the novels of James Baldwin, Toni Morrison, Pedro Lemebel, Léonora Miano, and Gabriel García Márquez, the poems of Teresa Calderón, Gabriela Mistral, and Pablo Neruda, the songs of Violetta Parra. To read essays about depression, then, and to look for other ones that approach depression differently, from elsewhere, from the margins where those less rich and less white live and express themselves, so that I may fulfill the need to make my racialized, diasporic, multilingual voice heard at the heart of this particular community, just as I do in other spaces: to show my mother's face and my own, my round face, my black hair, my hazel eyes, and my brown skin, so that depression may be more than just a rich white person thing. We too have a right to depression, to a depression that's our own, which is to say one that travels through history—colonialism, dictatorships, genocides, exiles, and racism. We too suffer, with the passion and fury ridiculously associated with us because of our rhythmic songs and our telenovelas which amuse though not without a certain contempt; we suffer with the passion and fury used against us to take away our right to suffer, to discredit our suffering, to reduce it to a simple cultural, exotic trait cleaved from our history like our gift for celebration and getting angry. *Passion, fury*:

rather than filling our depressed silence with these words, let's listen to it, let's hear this silence's eloquence, which brings to mind silences millennia in the making, silences to which we are still reduced because our celebrations and pop songs are so amusing they drown out the sobs of your janitors and cleaning women. Listen to and look at what's so particular about our depressions, the memory they reveal: *Memories of being snatched away by friend and stranger, stuffed into vessels that traversed vast spaces of water, chained, whipped, branded, hunted and sold by overlapping generational systems of degradation.* Our depressions recall the traumas of our ancestors, are performed just as our racialization is, just as our *brownness* which names the illness and symptoms in a different way, at times beneath what dominant and white epistemologies have developed as the pathological vocabulary of depression. *Depression is not brown, but there are modalities of depression that seem quite brown*, modalities that isolate our experiences and euphemize our condition; our depressions are further tenuous, further oblique, become *Latino maladies*—los nervios *and* attaques. To give them a shape of their own, we'll draw on our fictions, on our poems, on our folklore, so that we may cease to remain *beneath this illness*, so that our tongues, colours and subjectivities may make this illness their own. Our depressions are complicated because they originate not only in our experiences with discrimination, marginalization and racism but also in our own internalization of these conditions, of the racist gaze we lay on ourselves, of the words we repeat to invalidate our pains and to be part of the group that

Andrea Canaan
"Brownness"

José Esteban
Muñoz
"Feeling brown,
feeling down:
Latina affect, the
performativity
of race and
the depressive
position"

dominates us—*How often do we people of color place our necks on the chopping block?* What's more, we're attached to our depressions, because they're a form of agency: we're attached to our own forms of depression, to our own melancholy, because it's at once a trace and a consequence of our experiences with marginalization, a wound we drag along and a weapon we turn on our executioners. We're attached to our depression because it exists *for raced subjects both as a sign of rejection and as a psychic strategy in response to that rejection.* That's why our depression isn't the same as yours: el sufrimiento no es igual to suffering.

Gloria Anzaldúa
"La prieta"

Anne Anlin Cheng
The Melancholy of
Race: Psychoanalysis,
Assimilation, and
Hidden Grief

TO READ ESSAYS TO PLURALIZE MY DEPRESSION—to give it shapes that look like me, that correspond to the subjectivities with which I think and live and for which I have also suffered, essays that echo experiences of exclusion that in part made me who I am, that echo the violence of these rules, norms, and conventions I didn't know how to take on and from which I had to try, not without consequence, to emancipate myself. To diversify and decentre my readings to explore the *affective potential of queer*, so as to get away from the heterosexual norms underpinning a great many of the essays I was reading— the abundant mentions of spouses and children suffice to transform an interested reading into another experience of exclusion, into a reading made uncomfortable by heterosexuality, this system that *functions powerfully not only as a series of norms and ideals, but also through emotions that shape bodies as well as worlds.* These essays that sensitively study more or less marginal experiences are still decidedly located within a normative system that reserves its comforts only for *those who can inhabit it.* What's more, *queer subjects, when faced by the "comforts" of heterosexuality, may feel uncomfortable (the body does not "sink into" a space that has already taken its shape). Discomfort is a feeling of disorientation: one's body feels out of place, awkward, unsettled.* Studying literature got me

Sara Ahmed
The Cultural Politics of Emotion

Ahmed

Ahmed

87

used to making do with this discomfort, recognizing it and adopting the necessary positioning so that it doesn't impede my comprehension, doesn't become a wound, doesn't provoke the anger I nevertheless feel and have learned to contain from one reading to the next. However, this discomfort, like a kind of exasperation, always compels me to look elsewhere, to find other voices in order to read texts which, though they might fail to create a new comfort, name the contortions to which some of us must subject ourselves just to read, understand, reflect on, attempt to recognize ourselves—contortions of reading that are in fact contortions of our identities, means of invisibilizing ourselves, a skill queer folx have long mastered. This discomfort is etched onto our skin, gives it

Ahmed shapes we tame with resilience, provides us with an *acute awareness of the surface of one's body*, but it also gives rise to an embodied sensation of mental, psychic, psychological disorientation, itself compounded by a condition to which queer people must yield every day, both before and after

Ahmed coming out: *queer subjects may also be "asked" not to make heterosexuals feel uncomfortable.* The psychological effects of such discomforts, disorientations, and conditions are considerable, and often lead to the internalization of these heterosexual norms and requirements, to their reproduction within our communities and therefore to a novel form of assimilation which, paradoxically, will never be complete, will always be doomed to fail because, among other things, most of us live with the trauma of the closet, of rejection and of homophobia,

and battle the eternally haunting desire to turn away

from our old pain though it remains unforgettable: our suffering awakens the pain that scarred us, that had us hide our sexuality, and then celebrates it spectacularly by appropriating the abuses hurled at us and by drawing new languages out from the shame that colonizes our memory. And despite our astonishing ability to fend off our traumas by incorporating them into our struggles and our celebrations, sometimes we still end up a depressed minority, used to anticipating the rejection of our families, of our loved ones, of our classmates, of our work colleagues, but also the rejection of people within our own community because it's so codified, because it's a community made up of various relations of power, racism, ageism, masculinism, ableism, classism, misogyny, homonormativity, fatphobia, transphobia, oppressive beauty standards, and a multitude of other discomforts—

At times, I feel uncomfortable about inhabiting the word Ahmed *"queer," worrying that I am not queer enough, or have not been queer for long enough, or am just not the right kind of queer. We can feel uncomfortable in the categories we inhabit, even categories that are shaped by their refusal of public comfort.* Yes, sometimes we still end up a depressed minority, inclined to excesses (heavy drug use, anorexia, bigorexia, risky sex) which themselves are huge traps that may lead to, among other things, new rejection—an extra loop with devastating effects: social anxiety, emotional avoidance, detachment, self-rejection, depression, vicious circles born in the closet and which proceed, fuelled by unending anticipation of countless forms of rejection, as if self-hatred belonged to us, as if it were the

89

foundation on which to build our subjectivity, a hatred which doubles our shame—shame of being ourselves and shame of feeling shame. *The embarrassment of owning such feelings, out of place as they are in a movement that takes pride as its watchword, is acute.* Yes, sometimes we still end up a depressed minority, and paradoxically this queer political heritage to which we add our stories enables us to produce forms of hope that refuse to dismiss such different, negatively-regarded realities, realities from which queer subjectivities are constructed and which we come up against in our own communities. *The hope of queer politics is that bringing us closer to others, from whom we have been barred, might also bring us to different ways of living with others. Such possibilities are not about being free from norms […]. A queer hope is not, then, sentimental. It is affective precisely in the face of the persistence of forms of life that endure in the negative attachment of "the not." Queer maintains its hope for "non-repetition" only insofar as it announces the persistence of the norms and values that make queer feelings queer in the first place.* This queer hope is of course only possible if we take into account the circumstances of our emancipation from what formerly confined us—an emancipation made possible by the creation of communities wherein relations, sexuality, friendship, and family are re-evaluated—but avoiding denial is also crucial, which is to say that we have to acknowledge all that we won't ever fully escape, starting with the psychic, psychological damage wrought by rejection and heteronormativity. Queer hope doesn't deny the suffering at the origin of our stories, it lies in the

Ahmed

possibility of manipulating that suffering, of reshaping and reinvesting it within forms all our own. Transported, then, by this queer hope, our dazzling celebrations recognize our pride and visibility but also our differences, our bad memories, our night terrors, our traumas, our illnesses, our deaths, our losses, and our struggles. Our celebrations don't silence the pains that hound us. Our celebrations are histories, shows, stories, performances that provide us with an occasion to name our suffering and discomforts, to flaunt their mark on our bodies, on the old skin we so wish we could shed—I'm reminded of Arca's "Piel," of the wholly queer melancholy expressed when they sing *quítame la piel de ayer / no sé caer*—this skin we either choose to leave be or cover in sequins, because together we're free to recount our weaknesses, because together we can take care of each other. To read other essays, then, to blur the threshold between good and bad feelings, between joy and sadness, between pride and shame, between public and private—to put an end, in short, to binaries, and to take advantage of the potential held in stories of depression, the potential to encourage new affiliations. To read essays to situate my depression, racialized and queer, among the depressions of members of my communities, among the depressions of others, around which, together, we dance.

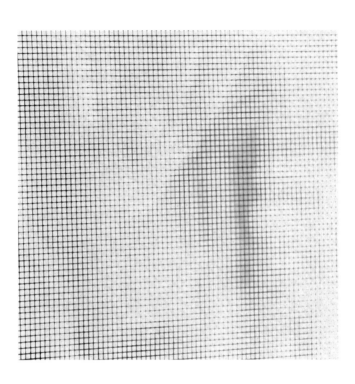

At la ventana, I address my tears from the night, my languages, my melancholic family airs. My words, intact and smooth, circle the earth and return exotic as the timbre of our suicided fathers, our defenestrated mothers. At la ventana, I scratch at the screen: a monotone guitar, a single note. And rising like songs, more specks of dust through which I can only make out cut-up, fragmented shards of a world whose sounds I forget. Una sola nota: the dust of languages at la ventana makes for a homogenous earth.

At la ventana, I try out a hymn that fails to burn the world down: I say *yo*, I wall myself in, I confine myself in fog—I shut up. I try my hand at a couple of images: I draw a flat place on the steamed-up surface, a field, earth beneath which our forebears lie, pero no pasa nada, nothing blows up. I haven't the courage of a kamikaze, my patience is my only weapon. Unrelenting, I choose to wait for the wind to blow its trenches so that it burns my dwelling, scatters the ashes of my voice, to the ground.

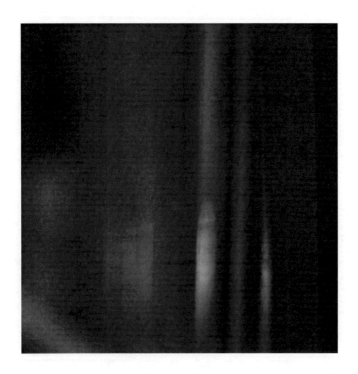

The way I remember it, chronology is out the door, I no longer know which outing precedes which, I have no idea if the one outing was on the same day as another, or how much time came and went in between: time no longer means much of anything, what matters instead is the outings, the discrepancy between systems into which we step when we get out of the house and the depressed state that confines me, confines me to my apartment and thus to myself, the confinement which foils every attempt at normal, natural communication with the external and the real, foils every appropriate reaction to the mechanics of social life, family, the medical world, the workplace. The way I remember it, I no longer know if this time out of the house is before or after having seen the doctor, before or after having found a therapist, before or after the first appointment with the acupuncturist, before or after my birthday; I no longer know if transit to my workplace by metro and bus goes smoothly, if the metro or bus is packed, if I sit or stand, if my too-old and too-thin coat has me hot or cold in this truly freezing winter, if I'm at peace with the day ahead of me, my last one at the college where I teach and where four students wait for me to deliver some bad news. I do, however, remember a conversation I had with one of them, a few months earlier, during rehearsals for a play we wrote together as part of an extracurricular project that was supposed to culminate with a trip to and staging of the play in France—a project I was leading and for which I had next to no skill but all the enthusiasm in the world, enthusiasm since reduced to nothing—I recall a conversation with one of them, with David, who pulled out of the project himself later on because he was overloaded, a conversation during which we talked about mental illness because David had confessed he didn't really get what burnout is. I remember him telling me *I think, when it comes down to it, it's just weakness*, I remember having an intense reaction to this claim that wasn't even directed at me, I remember even being a little aggressive and bringing up, as an example, a colleague who had recently confirmed her leave of absence for depression, I remember telling her story down to the tiniest details, revealing secrets she had entrusted to me, so that David and his friends could wrap their heads around how a depression can take on proportions that get the best of us and leave us completely unfit for work. The way I remember it, while walking toward the college, I tell myself *I should've known David was punishing his own weakness, I should've guessed that by talking about my colleague, I was talking about me.*

The way I remember it, I rush into the college's student café, I find them all there patiently waiting for me, and without ceremony or preamble, without taking my

97

coat off, without setting down my bags full of graded assignments, I give them the bad news, and Yann immediately answers *we get it, you know*, then Nerly adds *for sure, it's alright*, and Emmanuelle says *we could sort of tell, to be honest*, and Mélodie is quiet for a moment before saying, affectionately, *you don't have to apologize, you worked so hard*. I assure them, without knowing if it's true or not, that despite my absence the project won't fall by the wayside, and then I admit I've just made them an empty promise, and their laughter feels good, their listening and kindness make me want to cry, but I have to leave them in a moment to advise human resources and my colleagues that I'll be on leave. I no longer remember what comes next, I've erased the details of my announcement from my memory, I barely recall one colleague's *oh no* and the annoyance of another, mostly I remember a string of comments uttered in my direction that day, in the college's French department, a series of sentences I'll never forget: *I think I'm not doing so great either the semester's been a hard one there's so much work / oh yeah you can't tell though, you look like you're in great shape / I should go get a doctor's note too / you're better off at home this place is a mess / wow dropping like flies around here / so young and already tired you're not the strongest eh just kidding just kidding / don't come back mid-semester you'll piss your sub off / lucky fucker.*

The way I remember it, I say very little and everyone else responds all at once as if my announcement had been a question, and oddly enough their words don't really hit me; on the contrary, I feel endowed with an unwavering clarity, a sharp focus, an awareness fine enough to understand that these comments, these words that could hurt me, come from our incapacity for actual empathy, for empathy in real time, an incapacity undoubtedly caused by overwork, the anxiety of the semester's beginning, grading fatigue, the anguish we conceal with the smile we're forced to wear at that moment when we are expected, I have no idea why, to look forward to the coming months of tasks that pile up, weigh us down, that risk making us falter too, and I believe that I understand, with each of these comments that could hurt me, that it's fear talking, fear of being next, fear that empathy turns my face into this terrible mirror reflecting their own impending fatigue, their own potential depression.

The way I remember it, I leave the college revitalized, propelled by a strange energy, I tell myself *a rotten world left behind*, and I move forward into this other world, new as it is familiar, maybe just as rotten, where silence and confinement will make time unrecognizable, a world whose story, later, will only be tellable in constructed disarray.

TO READ ESSAYS ABOUT DEPRESSION—to remain excessively alert to all the everyday things we say about sadness, melancholy, feeling low, mental illness, suicide. To feel particularly afflicted by ready-made phrases and slogans—*Take a break, it'll do you good!* was the advice given that year, while I read William Styron, by the Canadian Mental Health Association, turning a social problem (excessive work hours, precarity, pressure, productivity demands, and competition in the workplace) into an individual one. *Take a break* would then not only be a sufficient remedy to curb mental illness but also an individual choice. Following such logic, the culprits would be the worker who didn't bother to *listen to their bodies*, the factory worker who didn't bother to *take care of herself*, those who didn't *take a break* at the right moment and who, with only themselves to blame, didn't bother to put an end to their terrible spiral toward *burnout, work-related fatigue, a leave of absence*. I became, as I read on, increasingly sensitive to this kind of euphemization and professionalization of mental health; I was reminded of my colleagues' reactions when I announced my depression, particularly the questions that followed, the *how come's*, the *why's*, questions we inevitably ask ourselves when we hear of the suicide of a person who, to our eyes, wasn't suffering: *That is why the greatest fallacy about suicide lies in*

the belief that there is a single immediate answer—or perhaps
combined answers—as to why the deed was done. That same
year, comedian Robin Williams, famous for his clownish
roles, took his own life. Though some people received the
news as an opportunity to start real conversations about
distress, a good number of people on social media stuck
to rather basic displays of heartbreak, to expressions of
surprise at the news that one of their childhood heroes, a
symbol of laughter and happiness, had taken the ultimate
step and in so doing revealed, in a baffling contradiction,
the secrets of his suffering. Others turned to the actor's
substance-abuse issues to explain his suicide, to prove
his laughter and love of life were perhaps, who knows,
the fruit of his intoxication, thereby inferring that a
depressed person stops having fun and laughing, that
they're done going for drinks with their friends, that they
don't take long strolls with their beloved, that they no
longer watch funny movies. The depressed person may
laugh less, may force it a bit more, they certainly have a
hard time experiencing pleasure naturally, but in reality
they're fighting to the last breath, they push for the
most resounding laughs to convince themselves they're
still in it, to stay in the game and, with their talent for
comedy, they even manage to make others laugh, to think
for a moment that they're doing better, that the illness
is fading, all while knowing deep down that it's all just
studied and repeated gestures they execute the same way a
mime plays inside an invisible remoteness. Alone in their
body, and so alone in the world, the depressed person
only has this funny kind of laughter to prolong their days   101

and try to soften the pain, this laughter to which they're still entitled even if it's no longer entirely theirs, seeing as they hear it like an echo which, instead of underscoring their love of life, now reveals the hole where they find themselves. The depressed person laughs like the clown cries; they see the lessons of Hollywood movies, some of them starring Robin Williams, as a scam. Laughter still exists, sure, but it doesn't shield them from suffering; it can even be a symptom of it, like shame, like anxiety, like anger—Styron, for instance, writes about the reproaches the poet Mayakovsky formulated against fellow poet Yesenin for killing himself (*which should stand as a caveat for all who are judgmental about self-destruction*), only to put an end to his own life a few years later. Among the artists who've committed suicide of whom Styron speaks, we find a good many whose works are nonetheless bright, colourful, beautiful, sometimes even comical; the author can't help but include himself in this tradition of melancholic artists as he recounts, with the help of literary and scientific references, the story of his own depression. If the forms of everyday life don't make us sensitive to the unutterable sufferings that drive the will to end one's life, maybe artforms—poetry, photography, stories, essays—succeed, for their part, in giving a voice, through our stories, to those who perished before us?

Styron

I press the tip of my index finger into the soft wood of the counter, I add the middle finger and slowly inch forward; my fingerprints latch on to the grain like a train I imitate, I say *choo-choo*, I say *choo-choo*. The sounds drag out of my body in quick puffs, jerky till the last *choo*, till the last train goes off the rails: my knees drag along the floor and my head rests on the corner of the countertop, I say *going off the rails, going off the rails*, I feel the corner of the countertop imprinting my forehead. I say *going off the rails*, right hand in the air, fingers nonchalantly sprawled out on the counter, left hand on the floor smushed up against my knee, and I can feel the corner of the countertop sinking deeper into my forehead and my left wrist seizing up on the floor; I keep an eye out for my pulse, I say *it's not moving anymore*. I say *cállense, cállense, déjense de gritar*. Help won't come because there is no help, I say *stop*, I say *stop screaming*, then I wait, hour after hour, for our puffing to wane, for our veins to wilt away. Hour after hour I wait: agony has made a patient man out of me.

In the centre of my forehead, right here, the imprint of the corner of the counter remains. I close my eyes to let the pain penetrate all the way to my brain, it becomes recurring, reassuring headaches, I say *my head hurts;* suddenly, I'm having fun, I clap my hands, I sing a chorus, a nursery rhyme, a slogan, I repeat *ay que me duele la cabeza, ay que me duele la cabeza,* and others are here, stuck in the kitchen with me, un coro solidario in shared pain. Our dancing feet kick up dead skin, crumbs, and dust, and we intone simple, efficient, intact words as smooth as the countertop that nevertheless still scrapes at our songs, to remind me that alone is here and siempre is now, día tras día, hour after hour. This headache: smoke and mirrors, a hymn brief as a corner.

GETTING OUT OF THE HOUSE: THERAPIST

The way I remember it, I lose my way on Saint Hubert Street because I keep repeating *this one's the one, this one's the one;* it sounds like a prayer I have no shame in declaiming aloud to myself despite the people around me, people who don't even look at me funny, accustomed as they are to all these people around the neighbourhood talking alone in the middle of the street, I tell myself *maybe this is what madness is,* I tell myself *so I'm crazy,* and all the while I repeat *this one's the one, this one's the one,* but I'm immediately disappointed when, in looking for the address, I realize this new therapist's office is in the half-basement of a building sandwiched between two youth hostels. The way I remember it, there's something grim about the idea of talking out my problems inside a sad cavern stuck between so many tourists celebrating their freedom.

The way I remember it, the entryway is stifling: the hall is so narrow as to force me to awkwardly make my way down the stairs sideways, to lean on a somewhat dirty wall featuring a few impersonal images of nondescript landscapes, flowers, fields, a sunset behind a mountain, I repeat *could be any fucking mountain,* then a message in

Times New Roman bold, on a sheet of legal-size paper, instructing visitors to leave their boots in the entryway. *Stinks of wet carpet,* I tell myself *smells like dirty slush.* At the end of the hall there's the waiting room, which is in reality just a few feet of wall equipped with a chair and a side table with a clock radio spitting out a midday show. The way I remember it, I hear a voice on the other side of the wall that blends with the radio host's yell-y, way-too-happy tone: *trente minutes de musique francophone sans interruption, ça c'est un vrai cadeau du midi, vous ne trouvez pas ?*[9] There's nothing to look at in this windowless, depthless waiting room, just a closed door that'll soon open, and the clock radio I stare at, transfixed by the sounds blasting out of it, these upbeat piano licks, these cheerful harmonies, these songs as naïve as nursery rhymes. There's nothing else to do, in this waiting room, but listen too closely to these bits of music that bring nothing to mind, offer up nothing to explore, nothing but simplistic lyrics and stories too tragic for such melodies: *car même l'ennui / et même la mort / ne viennent pas ici / dis-moi si j'ai tort / on est dans la nuit / et toi dans mon corps / oublions nos vies / réécrivons l'histoire.*[10] I listen to the words like one reads poems, I think this song could make a good jingle for this therapist's office: the upbeat mood of the tune tells us of the necessity to erase a sad and heavy past to create a new story exempt from death and boredom, and yet I think to myself *this is taking forever this is boring somebody kill me.* It's true that this kind of song bores me to death, same as the one that comes on next, a happy breakup song, a fake casualness about the imminent departure of an unfaithful lover, amidst a chorus that desperately constrains every line to an ain rhyme sung in an unbearable accent—I think *but who even talks like that?* Time wears on and the hook pulls me into a strange loop that gets in my head and won't get out: *mais dis-moi adieu demain / mais dis-moi adieu en chemin / va voir les autres je n'en pense rien / je t'ai aimé mais je t'assure que c'est la fin.*[11]

The way I remember it, I realize in that exact moment, on the umpteenth repetition of *je t'assure que c'est la fin,* that I arrived at the therapist's office way too early, and this wait, which could've been a relaxing time, becomes an anxious one instead, so I become obsessed with the clock radio I can't take my eyes off of, as if every minute that passes is a stage cleared, a feat in itself, an obstacle overcome in view of my redemption, as if each song, each hook, each lyric, each rhyme is transforming itself into a poem to empty out and a slogan to my torment, to my wait, to my state, to my pathetic search for a therapist, to all my time out of the house: *allez on va danser / au bar des suicidés / comme autrefois on gardera les yeux fermés / allez on va danser / au bar des suicidés / laisse tes pas un à un devant toi s'aligner.*[12]

The way I remember it, these are the lyrics that bounce around inside me—*oublions nos vies, je t'assure que c'est la fin, au bar des suicidés*[13]—as I tell the story of my illness to the new therapist. As I leave the office, my head full of words and songs I don't like and that now crowd, occupy, overrun my memory, I repeat, yielding and resilient, *this one's the one.*

I gaze at my reflection in the fork's glint, I say *four little tips, metallic and gleaming*, I say *makeshift diamonds, nuggets for glass-cutting*. I then try for a little sensuality and bring them up to my mouth so that they hook onto my tongue, cut into my palate, gloss my lips with a lusciousness that could trickle down my neck and drip all over the counter like a hanging body. I'd be nothing but astride: a mass of bloodied flesh, four wounds, four dazzling stabs at scarification.

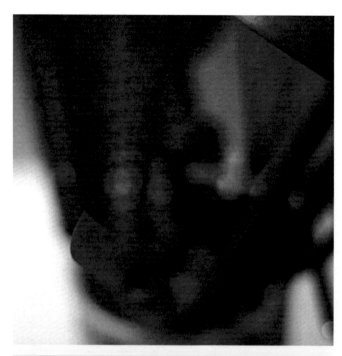

Peppercorns on the table, I say *I could, I can…* I don't finish my sentence. The fruit change colour in the bowl, the condiments encrust the wood. At the table, I smell nothing, I see nothing but the letters of the words I utter, *puedo, quiero…* Rot and fruit flies tickle my nose, I know it, *si lo puedo,* I should… but sitting there at the table, I see a wall, splatters and unrecognizable fruit, stains blending in a paralyzing slowness. Para ver, para hacer, I have to get my head under the table, so I say *quiero, debo,* and suddenly my head rests against the chair leg. Here, the smell is metal, dust, and a painful blend of foods, of leftovers I hear in agony. *Here it stinks,* I say *everything finishes itself off, here everything goes dead.* This is where I live.

I open the refrigerator door with a trembling arm, I hold my breath: I fear the old flavours—cafecito, heladito, chocolate. I discover one more room there, a bedroom, new walls gleaming and cold gleamingly, coldly shameless. I try foods to warm myself up a bit, I say *pan, lechuga, jugo, queso, leche.* I keep the list going, I name what isn't there, a couple of exotic fruits and elaborate dishes, then I say *shelf, glass, plastic.* I name myself, I say *oven, cupboards, drawers, china cabinet.* The list, día tras día, carries on beyond the fridge, things filled with things among things filled with things, within this kitchen that contains me. My head chills, next to a cauliflower I address: *I'm the end, I'm empty,* I say *no te preocupes, no te comeré.*

TO WRITE ESSAYS NOT ONLY ABOUT DEPRESSION but first and foremost about a process of research and creation in order to avoid recounting the depressive episode and the months-long leave of absence—depression is a trip that can't be recounted without calling up memories, impressions, reflections, theories, sciences, and works one by one; the story of the hurt then turns into study, chronicle, analysis, inquiry, notebooks, journal, fragments. Depression quietly metamorphoses in front of you, by you, into a hybrid and malleable thing outside of yourself, a thing you move, paragraph by paragraph, alongside everything you can conjure up so that the past, the experiences, and the ideas converse. Without these conversations, memory, so splintered by the shockwaves of depression, remains mute. *Trauma* Hustvedt *memory has no narration. Stories always take place in time.* And depressive time is a time that fails like language fails you, like words fail you. It's not altogether possible, then, to recount depression (I don't discuss it much with those I'm close to because, among other reasons, the feeling of inexactitude that accompanies such discussions is unbearable—I always think *that's not quite it, I'm making things up here, I'm obscuring things there*), that is, to align the different times the depression has isolated to make a single one, that of the story. Better to make visible the

115

borders, the ruptures, the divides between excruciatingly fragmented times, along with the efforts deployed to give them meaning and distance without denying, without disappearing, the suffering they provoke. To do it in the construction—you could call it *fiction*: pictures, poems, stories, essays.

The way I remember it, the sessions with the therapist—
this one's the one—are all the same: the walk down to her
basement is always just as cold, the wait with the clock
radio is always just as tiresome, the songs that get into
my head are always just as inane, and the therapist's
smile is always just as fake. Each session gets under way
with her hands gathered under her chin, and each time
I'm surprised by the sight of her lumpy arthritic fingers,
I tell myself she must be well into her sixties, that you
wouldn't know it if it wasn't for these lumpy arthritic
fingers, then I'm embarrassed by this domineering,
sexist thought, so at every session, tangled up in my own
repetitive, inappropriate line of thinking, I struggle to
get going, I struggle to speak, I don't ever know what
to talk about, and most of the time that's exactly what I
say, *I don't know what to talk about,* and without knowing
how, I suddenly begin to speak. Often, I stop and
become strangely incapable of looking her in the eye, I
contemplate the carpet while waiting for something new
to say, and sometimes she talks to me, she finds the right
words to keep me telling my story, to get me to change
the subject, or to get back to a story I abandoned during
a previous session, but through no fault of her own she'll

always fail to put me at ease, because I'll never be the kind of patient who manages an intimate rapport with their therapist, and it's no doubt better this way: I'm always too skeptical of and allergic to power imbalances to allow myself to be drawn into such a relationship, I prefer uneasiness, hesitancy, the awkwardness we seem to nestle into each session, and maybe I find a certain comfort in this discomfort that keeps me from crying in front of my therapist like the patient that precedes me does every week, the one who blubbers so noisily I hear her through the door while I wait not altogether without jealousy, while I endure the pop songs of Quebec bursting with a happiness that punctuates the sobs and sniffling of this patient whose face I've never seen because she hides it with her hair every time she comes out of our therapist's office.

The way I remember it, I made up countless horror stories for this patient, this blubberer, stories of breakups, of losses, of heartbreaking departures, of a terrible childhood, and of illness, but I've forgotten all of them.

The way I remember it, I recount anecdotes from my childhood, from my past, from that solitude I felt when I shut myself in my room to write poems and draw in a sketchbook with experimental electronic music in the background, and the therapist breaks her silence to unsettle me: *every time you talk about this period from your childhood it's as if you're talking about today.* I stare at the carpet, she says *maybe you suffered from depression as a kid.*

I stare at the carpet, she says *think about it, keep it in mind,* *we won't be digging into your childhood today. Tell me about* *your sleep, are you still having a hard time sleeping? Tell me* *about your nights.* I look at the carpet, I say *yeah, no, I'm* *still not sleeping, very little, for months I've been having* *nightmares when I sleep, and otherwise, no, not sleeping, not* *really.* She gives me a meditation trick I don't really get, she tells me to gaze at the doorknob and think about this, then think about that, then about this again, then about that, and to listen to my breathing, to focus my attention on my body, its tensions, its pains, its numbnesses, then to let my eyes close without forcing them, and to again think about this, about that, it all seems complicated to me, I pretend to get it, I play at enthusiasm perfectly, she looks satisfied, I think *I shouldn't lie to my therapist,* and she no doubt gathers from my face that her trick won't work for me, that I'm not convinced, so she recommends consulting an acupuncturist, *it can do miracles, absolute* *miracles.* She has this habit of repeating herself, same as I do, we fill up blank space, amidst the awkwardness, with what's already been said. *You look skeptical, you've never* *tried it?* I look at the carpet, I say, *yeah, no, I am skeptical,* *never tried.* She gathers her lumpy fingers under her chin, I say *I'll try, I'll try.* I think *another time out of the house,* I repeat *I'll try.*

Without enthusiasm, I bring bread, water, an apple up to my mouth; I think and forget; my mouth, between my glistening tongue and concrete palate, locks old air away. ¿Qué he comido? The bread, water and apple are still whole on the counter: I start over. I eat a slice, I drink, I bite into, I talk with my mouth full: *tastes like an open field,* I say *tastes like ploughing.* I feed on dregs and debris, on wood, on broken glass, on my own blood. I swallow, I expel, I start over, día tras día, hour after hour. It knots up my stomach, my tongue, en el aire ahogado de mi boca, in the kitchen's stale air; and the food, untouched, keeps rotting on the counter.

The way I remember it, I wait a good hour before the acupuncturist comes into the clinic all sweaty. I have no idea why I imagined a tall, rugged man, maybe because his name has a Slavic ring to it, but I'm surprised, though neither relieved nor disappointed, when I see a rather young man, small and stocky, with this lost and hurried look on his face—like a student bursting into class an hour late. He calls my name and doesn't apologize for his lateness, I shoot him an annoyed look, I say *I've been waiting an hour, is that the usual? It's my first time, I'm not sure how this works,* he answers *no, not typical, got mixed up, sit down, what needs releasing?* He nervously lays out his tools on the table, opens the file, pulls out a form, writes down the date, drops his pen, picks it back up, scribbles a few bits of information I can't quite make out, all while sweat keeps rolling down his forehead, and he keeps breathing at a runner's pace, and his hands are shaking. I hand him the acupuncture prescription from my doctor, which reads *depression—acupuncture—1-2x/week.* He takes hold of the paper, doesn't read its contents, makes do with looking over its surfaces, the front, the back, and wrinkling it a bit with his thumb, he says, *what's this,* I don't answer, I don't know how to react anymore, I wanted him to be a tall, rugged man with a deep, calm voice who would address me softly, secretively, carefully, and benevolently, a man who would know how to relax and extricate me, by the tip of his needles at the tip of his fingers, from this state which now reduces me to silence. *What needs releasing?* He has a nasally, grating voice, a fitful tone, he never looks me in the eye, and the sweat on his forehead keeps dripping, and his shaking hasn't stopped: I say *it's written right there, depression.* He plops his pen down on his files to signal his annoyance, and looks me in the eye for the first time: *physical, not mental. What needs releasing?*

The way I remember it, all my physical symptoms, in a matter of seconds, are imprinted in my mind, one atop the other in a scrawl, a blackened mess, a stain, and I wish I could, right this instance, reproduce the violence of this stain as sound, as a scream, to force this acupuncturist to experience this stain as a hideous wail that'll never leave him, that'll weigh on him whenever he hears the unpleasant sounds of daily life, motors, jackhammers, too-high voices, nails on a chalkboard, but I keep myself from screaming, because in reality the sounds that come out of me are still so faint, don't imitate my fury, so, with a discouraged sigh, I simply, calmly say *insomnia.*

The way I remember it, I'm laid out under the air vent while he pokes me here and there, leaves me alone in the room for a while, comes back, pokes me again, goes off again, comes back, pokes me again, goes off again; 123

each needle transfers a bit more of his nervousness, his shakiness, his forehead sweat, his annoyance, a bit of all of it to me, moreover I feel an intense pain in the spot he sticks a particular needle, I have a hard time telling him when he comes back, I do so without confidence, without will, subject to his whim, reduced to the role assigned to me, here beneath the air vent, poked all over, beset and on my own, left to my own devices with this needle which hurts like a dagger and which he pulls out without a word, in a quick, sharp gesture, then he repeats the same procedure, the same quick and sharp gesture, to remove the other needles. I no longer recognize my body, which seems riddled with holes, strewn with cavities and craters that I'll have to count in the night like counting sheep while waiting for sleep to come. He says *we're done, if you still can't sleep come back next week, same time.*

The way I remember it, I go back a few times, then I abruptly stop seeing him, without telling him, without warning, without apologizing for my sudden absence. No doubt he'll think me cured, though in reality I'll only get back to sleep many months later, I don't know how, thanks to whom, thanks to what; at first I go to the other extreme, I sleep fourteen, sixteen hours, and then slowly, night by night, nightmare by nightmare, my sleep will become a bit more normal, though always a little fog-like, always a little precarious, often crowded with images of hole-riddled bodies and pitted flesh, but all the same sleep that resembles what we mean when we say *I slept well.*

Out of breath, I say *this is the end,* in a scratchy voice, worn out by injuries. Time speaks inside me: fleeting, my sentences linger on like war. The hall is a sap I get through on my elbows, on my stomach; I scrape my cheeks, I swallow stone and I lie down midway, at the centre of the trench and amidst the gunfire, the explosions, the screams, then with the quiet after the attack, this silence that kills its wounded and counts its dead, this vast silence I rip with a wail: I mutter nonsense que se parece al dolor; I've vanquished nothing, I say *la lucha será* once more. A forest, a clearing and a city in ruins around me, impenetrable barricades separate the kitchen from the living room, the living room from the bedroom. Broken, día tras día, *I'd like to desert,* I repeat to myself without a sound, no digo nada más. Walled in, my voice mangled as bones: a phantom limb.

Every night I crawl to bed, counting the specks of dust along the way: concrete, skin, palabras I believed had the power to change las ventanas en cielo y los muros en campos. But *time speaks inside me*, I say it again. A tautological time utters words that can't keep me away from my bed, which I dutifully locate in the torment, every night, like a spectre regaining its coffin. Dutifully, a good soldier, I review the day's horrors: limbs and trails of blood, humiliating prayers addressed to the light. I cling to the edge of the bed until night repeats itself and plunges me, hour after hour, into dread of this unseemly sun: again tomorrow, it will pierce the curtain and light yesterday's pictures.

TO WRITE ESSAYS so as to get out of the house, given that *explicit memories thrive on places,* like the memories of the feeling of constant confinement that overwhelmed me inside my apartment—these places come first in the story I recount. It's what depression did to such places: to transform, to unhinge the way I look at them, pushing me to regard them, starting with my own dwelling, like I used to perceive my body—that is, as a prison. Classic symptom but no less a tragic one, because it kicks you out even as it shuts you away. *Dans ce drame de la géométrie intime, où faut-il habiter?*[14] Maybe you have to start over, to rebuild your dwelling, to invest in a fiction, then, to build a new place. Indeed, it's the picture-taking that freed me up, these interior wanderings, the production of images of my apartment, as if a first step in a long process, often interrupted, of distancing myself from the walls—of my body, of the house, of the illness— that were shutting me in, and that made any recourse to language, to narrative, to sense-making impossible. Would healing from depression then perhaps coincide with an extraordinary moment wherein, for the good of creating, the memory that causes suffering calls on the imaginary, and vice versa / and the imaginary on the memory? *Ainsi, en abordant les images de la maison avec le souci de ne pas rompre la solidarité de la mémoire*

Hustvedt

Bachelard

Bachelard

127

et de l'imagination, nous pouvons espérer faire sentir toute l'élasticité psychologique d'une image qui nous émeut à des degrés de profondeur insoupçonnés. Par les poèmes, plus peut-être que par les souvenirs, nous touchons le fond poétique de l'espace de la maison.[15] But every house has walls, no matter how poetic they may be: to write poems about the house as I used to see it was also to return to confinement, to get back to a house of suffering, despite the ventanas, ancestros, idiomas, horizontes. That's the risk of poetry, and that's maybe also why the poem is so close to the essay: like opposites, they're drawn to each other, and switch roles as needed to help each other out. When one's wings are singed, the other moves it back from the fire; when the other can't get off the ground, the one lifts it up into the air. When poems became another prison, one of words and images, the essay came to the rescue by reminding me that, on the other side of the door, there was a community waiting to be read, to be reread, ready to have every conversation in the world with me. So, to write essays to name the words, to speak the pain because *ce mal, il est indispensable qu'on le traite, qu'on le soigne et, surtout, qu'on le dise, qu'on l'exprime. Qu'on se mette en face de lui et qu'on le reconnaisse : oui, c'est toi, chose glauque et verdâtre qui vient ruiner mes nuits.*[16] It's a question of literal movement: to move yourself to get the pain moving, to strip it of its negative energy and free it from its walls, to no longer think of depression as a dead end: *If depression is conceived of as blockage or impasse or being stuck, then its cure might lie in forms of flexibility or creativity more so than in pills or a different*

Labro

128

genetic structure. [...] Defined in relation to notions of blockage or impasse, creativity can be thought of as a form of movement, movement that maneuvers the mind inside or around an impasse, even if that movement sometimes seems backward or like a form of retreat. Spatialized in this way, creativity can describe forms of agency that take the form of literal movement.

Cvetkovich
Depression: A
Public Feeling

The ceiling, the bed, the floor—between them, in the dark, my body and mouth just as flat; laid out on my stomach, on my back, on my side, I'm just another surface in this heap of stacked surfaces. I open my mouth, fail to muster the voices ringing in my ears; es que no entiendo la esperanza y no reconozco el dolor. My flat muteness is scattered across the airwaves, crushed at the dead centre of an unstable device. Awakening joins my troubles like a refrain: arms numb, stiff neck, head thumping, chest tight, all ruins whose cacophony plunges me into a sudden night, a startled sleep that is nothing but empty, coma, black with nowhere to grip. When I wake up, I'll think *my words are destroyed once more.* I'll think *esta noche canté pero hoy de nuevo I'll collapse.*

TO WRITE STORIES because the house has doors, an obvious fact I used to consider impossible, and when the poems and essays were set down in writing, confinement wasn't the only thing reproduced, there was also the fear I might create a thing that doesn't tell the truth, that hides all these times out of the house that punctuated the depression and played an important role in the times and spaces of the depressive experience, because these times out of the house weren't by any means times outside of myself, weren't occasions for happy strolls or for recentring; on the contrary, they were moments of intense vulnerability which, most of the time, reinforced the walls of my dwelling because they consigned me to a series of systematic processes, obligations, and situations that disregard the subject's physical, affective, and emotional state, that objectivize suffering, that have the power to dispossess us of our own situation even as we must still, somehow, take said situation in hand. Strangely, it was during these monthly and weekly outings that I believed I was healing, that I regained a taste for words and images; it was also when I collapsed on the sidewalk, as I believed myself healed, that I slowly came to understand I'd need a lot of time to make it through this illness and to find the most appropriate shapes to give the stories of my experience, shapes that don't consider this experience as being isolated from those I lived through or inherited (the Chilean dictatorship, the assignment of gender roles amidst questions of familial affect, the transmission of the trauma of exile, the racism, the construction of an identity and of a sexual orientation, the coming-out, the homophobia, my relationships, my time in university, my artistic practices, my social mobility, my privileges, etc.) but rather as resonating with those experiences, the better to propose means of recounting and theorizing the self that also engage collective and political phenomena. This personal story is then also a story of outings: writing stories, essays, and poems, taking pictures of the house to extricate myself from the systems that confine me to it, to get far enough from the house and to observe, amidst my loves, the fires, floods, worksites, and renovations at the heart of my communities, then to head back to the house to create anew, to return to the swells of depression and its emotions that move us, to invest the positive energy of depression by celebrating its suffering and its various inheritances—to create. There it is, depression's basic lesson. Creating is a way of moving. Creating is a way to move around impasses that weigh us down, an occasion to solve riddles, to encourage thinking, to breathe meaning and pleasure into the present. Creating is a multitude of processes, it's to loop around what we live, to tinker, night after night, with our stories, our images, our readings, and our writings, to produce scraps with which, when the sun comes up, we can keep playing, keep moving, keep taking pictures, keep writing stories, essays and poems so that we may, once again, get out of the house.

GETTING OUT OF THE HOUSE: THERAPIST

The way I remember it, you can hear spring coming, at least that's what people are saying, the rumour circulating, same as every year this too-long winter devastates moods, occupies people's thoughts, dominates conversations, but winter isn't what's dragging on, it's the illness, to which I've grown exasperatedly accustomed like we get used to the cold despite desperate prayers for warmth to return. I do remember, however, that trips to the therapist's office are no longer quite as tiresome, are a bit more sprightly, and I start to wonder if it's not the simple promise of spring that speeds up my gait and makes me a bit more attentive to what's under way outside, to the sound of grey snow mixing in with bits of gravel under my feet, to the sound of icicles dripping, to this musical and stubborn slowness with which winter melts away and which makes people so antsy, sometimes prickly, whereas I gradually start to hear life unfolding on the other side of my window and I get the feeling, little by little, that I'm part of it. The way I remember it, I don't trust the phrases I'm somehow excitedly starting to hear myself think: *soon I'll be better / I slept last night / that smells good / that tastes good / I remember time as it goes by.*

The way I remember it, I talk to the therapist about all this, I'm embarrassed about it, I wonder aloud if I haven't lost my mind and I can't tell, as if I've lost my legs yet I'm convinced I'm walking, persuaded of my healing, of my deliverance, ready to throw it all up in the air for a few hopeful days, and I also bring up the fear that comes after the hope, fear of a bad night, of waking up captive to an even more debilitating despair now doubled over by grief for hope lost yet again. I begin to figure out that this fear, which my therapist reveals to me in a single solemn sentence—*that's anxiety, you know this*—that this fear won't leave me again: I'll learn to live with it, to recognize it, to sometimes avoid it, to tame it, most of the time, with an exhausting resilience, to let it take up what space it must, to let it indulge in its fits and spectacles, then pick up the broken pieces and continue the normal course of my life with this threat I'll learn, paradoxically, to love. I tell the therapist that these suddenly positive phrases which cautiously impose themselves on me and which I don't trust because of the anxiety, that this new hope which delights and scares me, is all due to the promise of spring, of the sun about to reappear. I say *I'll be walking again soon.* She says *you're already walking.* She says *picture yourself travelling, picture yourself walking abroad, in another country, say... Spain.*

The way I remember it, I get what she's telling me, which has nothing to do with the advice of that Wolfe Street therapist, she's not simply suggesting a trip to a warm country because of sun and dance; she's suggesting I try getting out again, getting out of the house in a more radical way, to help me evaluate how I'm doing, now propelled by the hope of a new spring and even of a better world. I get it because she adds *does that scare you?* I don't quite answer, I shrug my shoulders, I think *yeah I'm scared,* and days or months later I'll decide to mock that fear by booking plane tickets to Madrid, to Valencia. I'll believe myself victorious, the sun will be mine; I'll forget to think about the anxiety already settled within me.

TO CREATE—to imagine stories of depression and make them line up with those other stories that already make me up, to formulate yet another diaspora to belong to, because diasporas that, in their dispersal, bring together people from a common country, speaking a common language, raised in a common religion and having similar experiences of exile, in turn bring about additional, less easily identifiable diasporas, spaces of affect within which we are many coming together in a strange silence I'd like to break. To get out of the house, to leave a country, to acclimatize to a new culture and new languages, to belong little by little to something much more elusive, moving, and precarious than a single country, what we sometimes call the in-between, exile, or migration—all of that provokes feelings of loss, places grief at the centre of our experiences, within an oscillation between nostalgia and melancholy; these feelings are part of a diasporic culture that may be transmitted, often unconsciously, from one generation to the next, another thing that makes racialized people, people from displaced families, seek each other out, back each other up. Basically, I delve into this depressive experience with the goal of giving new shapes to this diaspora of affect to which we belong, we exiles from every country who carry wide-ranging stories of travel and family, who carry loss within us like *a series of unresolved fragments, we come together as a contingent whole. We gain social recognition in the face of this communal loss.* Together, we make up a diaspora of affect that also contributes to rethinking nationalism, the one and same which, with its noise and pride, drowns out more sensitive and precarious voices, this nationalism that turns its back on the pain and suffering for which it is, at least in part, responsible. To create, then, so as to propose a multiple, plural, hybrid story, in the image of this diaspora that celebrates, in the disarray of grief, loss, melancholy, and other feelings we deem negative, a story that takes these feelings as a given and which, armed with this agency, attempts to combat the nationalist mania that pushes people to flee pain at all costs, to get rid of all forms of fragility, to cancel it, to control it, to pathologize it, to marginalize it, to put it in boxes in order to create reassuring categories that serve to build, box by box, what they call a nation—this is what I see, what I hear, when I'm asked to choose one country or the other, one language or the other, when I'm told that a return to my roots will do me good, will get me back to my truth, and when I'm told, inversely, that I'm a real Quebecer, that I speak without an accent, that there's no difference between us, that my lack of clear memories of my Chilean childhood safeguards me from nostalgia, and therefore from madness, that the psychological and affective consequences of exile shouldn't afflict me because I might as well have been born in Quebec, seeing as my assimilation has been such an obvious success, has so obviously healed me. This assimilation didn't heal me, no more than did the nation that naturalized me and of which I'm a citizen today, a nation which nevertheless routinely reminds me I don't quite belong to it because I wasn't born in it, and which doesn't care to recognize the diasporas to which I belong. This is how, from generation to generation, *the trauma of immigration continues, and it's why the trauma of immigration need not be "healed" by a return to the "natural" nation of origin or assimilation into a new one* [...]. *Both the fantasy of return to an origin and the desire to assimilate can be strategies for forgetting the trauma of dislocation. The emphasis here, by contrast, is on the possibility that acknowledging traumatic loss can be a resource for creating new cultures,* different, alternative cultures that require hybrid, interdisciplinary and decentralized forms to truly translate the plurality of means by which we experience displacement, belonging, and identity. For me, this is a decidedly queer process, one which relies not only on my experiences with migration and racialization but also on my queer subjectivity, with which I invest loss, rejection, and other traumatic forms of marginalization, that is, what are normally seen as negative experiences to be left behind and never gone through again, in order to positively make possible the creation of less hegemonic and less binary means of speaking (ourselves) and of creating (ourselves), and to potentially contribute to the formation of more sensitive communities whose members do not deny the pain that brings them together: *Queer or nonnormative forms of cultural reproduction open up possibilities for constructing cultural loss as something other than traumatic*

Cvetkovich
An Archive of Feelings: Trauma, Sexuality, and Lesbian Public Cultures

or irretrievable loss. Here there's also the political part of
the experience of depression that I desperately create, by
any means possible, whether written or pictured, reflexive
or creative, prosaic or poetic. Depression is in fact made
up of successive temporalities: a time for despair, a time
for quiet, a time for self-destruction, a time for lightness,
incredulity and cynicism, a time for denial, hope, relapse
and failure, a time for exhaustion and hypersomnia, a
time for hyperactivity and insomnia, a time for paranoia
and hypochondria, a time for mediation, weighing the
past, and nostalgia, a time for isolation, anxiety and
confinement, a time for laughing and rejoicing, times
always in disarray, sometimes simultaneously. But for
those who don't lose their life to depression, for those
who aren't engulfed by it, there's also a time for coming
out of depression, and for me, this time has been
paradoxically accompanied by the return of depressive
symptoms because I sought them out myself by revisiting
this experience, by getting back to it thanks to images,
by reshaping it with essays, stories, poems, photographs.
This time is the one when I take depression down from
the pedestal of illness, the pedestal of pathology that
confines depression to a glass cage to observe its signs,
symptoms, causes, and consequences like we look over
relics in a museum, in order to move it into the active,
plural, unstable and collective sphere of the political. *The*
goal is to depathologize negative affects so that they can be
seen as a possible resource for political action rather than as
its antithesis.

The way I remember it, I'm no longer wearing my too-thin winter coat but rather a black raincoat with a collar that makes it look like a smock. As always, I've left the house too early for my monthly doctor's appointment, but this time I take my time walking over so I can take in the sun which, while not truly warming the city up, not yet, does make our strolls happy ones: people smile at each other as they cross paths.

The way I remember it, I still don't quite trust this new lightness, I still can't easily distinguish furtive hopes from real healing, later on I will figure out that we're never really fully healed from depression, never so quickly, and that this kind of experience changes everything ahead of us, even the sunniest spring.

The way I remember it, this time my doctor isn't scared to ask how I'm doing. Like everybody else, he brings up the weather, the lengthy, hard winter we just had. He's suspicious, though, of this thaw, late though it may be, he says *you never know in Quebec, a storm can always surprise us.* I share in his cautiousness, I don't yet feel ready to talk about this winter in the past tense. He adds *you're looking*

141

well. I say *yeah, but I'm scared of the next storm.* He hands me the questionnaire I now know by heart, I know this appointment will be the last one. As I fill it out, he jokes around: *you look like a doctor, a stylish one, in that coat.*

The way I remember it, I'm not afraid as he looks my answers over, but I'm still anxious, I think *I don't want to come back here.* He smiles a big smile, he tells me *you don't need me anymore, I hope I don't ever see you again.* I pretend to laugh, his joke annoys me. Despite our monthly appointments we still aren't any closer, our relationship won't ever shake off the roles we gave each other at my first appointment: I'm the quiet, frightened patient, he's the expeditious doctor doing his best. Humour between us isn't quite right, is out of place, insulting, and that's a shame, surely, seeing as humour, these past many months, never managed to carve out a place for itself among the questionnaires, forms, prescriptions, and lists of symptoms. From now on, this place and this man will remain stuck in the recess of my memory that collects the darker stories, those I'll somehow spend my life reformulating.

The way I remember it, he tells me to soak up the sun. I tell him I'm actually planning a trip to Spain, and as soon as I say it I'm embarrassed I'm playing his game, giving in to this lightness to which we feel beholden because of the sun and this victory we're celebrating before we should. He seems uneasy, awkwardly rejoicing: *take care of yourself over there. The battle's never over.*

Under my eyelids, the storm still. Ship, raft, rowboat: the mattress capsizes. I roll up in my sheets and dive under to save myself. I lie on the floor a long while, gaze at the concrete, drifting in time. I say *what will my next moves be?* Exhausted, I open my eyes, I say *the bed sinks, the ceiling heaves.* I recount my nightmares to a mirror that holds my breath: they turn to fog, steam, become a breath from another time. They fit me like a glove and turn inside out, make for a deleterious night and turn the day upside down. The waves now mix awake and asleep, hold me on the edge of open sea in an endless daybreak.

GETTING OUT OF THE HOUSE: VALENCIA

The way I remember it, Valencia isn't a city, it's an aftershock. The facts are as follows: I left Montreal in top shape, I wandered around Madrid with a series of signs of a setback that all quickly converged toward a stunning case of tonsillitis, I arrived in Valencia exhausted, convalescent and, above all else, anxious. The way I remember it, everything I'd loved about Spain till then irritates me in Valencia—the scorching sun, the noise, the graffiti, the linguistic diversity, the mealtimes, the party vibe I'm not part of. I start sleeping over ten hours a night again, regretful and embarrassed I've let Valencia slip through my fingers while I curl up in this apartment sandwiched between a train station and three construction sites. I get out regularly, though, to take advantage of the beach, to visit museums and interesting neighbourhoods, even to attempt to talk to other people at a bar and a park, but all of that takes place in more or less happy intervals between moments when anxiety makes the hours rush past and the events slippery, whether important or banal. The way I remember it, the nights are long because they're dedicated to erasing the content of the days that precede them.

The way I remember it, overcome with panic set off by I no longer remember what undoubtedly banal event, I spend a night in a crisis of which I only retain the briefest memories and which I manage to mitigate by buying overpriced train tickets to Barcelona for the next day, then a plane ticket from Barcelona to Berlin to join my partner. When I arrive at the airport, he puts his hand between my shoulder blades. The anxiety remains, doubled over by a shame I can't name that'll erase the rest of my memories of this abridged time in Spain, but I think to myself *at least I'm no longer alone.* We won't talk much about what happened in Valencia, instead we'll take advantage of Berlin with that lovers' idleness which, oddly enough, is no stranger to caution. Berlin will make gifted tightrope-walkers out of my partner and me: we'll walk on eggshells and construct every bit of quiet needed to keep me on top of this tenuous high wire of stability. My trust will be complete, as will his diligence. That hand on my back, between my shoulder blades, will be the loveliest memory from my depression.

The way I remember it, I'll live with the shame of it all for years to come, ashamed that I thought myself invincible after barely a few months of this illness, ashamed also of my privileges, of the means to not only get as far out of the house as Spain but also to abruptly shorten the trip. These are fortunate circumstances many don't benefit from, starting with my parents, stuck as they were, those first years of exile, despite a deep melancholy, stuck on this unknown, strange, sometimes inhospitable soil with children to raise, new languages to learn, and strangers' toilets to scrub. Since this setback in Valencia, I've started to feel ashamed of all my travelling, and this shame will, sometimes contemptuously, make a place for itself in the story of my illness and in my travelogues; today I don't think there's any harm in shame if it decentres us.

Years later, I'll read a friend's novel featuring suicide and restless wandering in Valencia. *Claire Halde quitte Valence sans savoir si elle y reviendra un jour. Cette ville lui résiste. Elle parvient difficilement à s'y orienter. Sa géographie semble tourner le dos à la mer. […] Elle s'est perdue dans cette ville beaucoup plus qu'ailleurs dans le monde. Même au moment où le train quitte la gare, elle ne peut pas dire où se trouvent le nord, le sud, dans quelle direction sont Barcelone ou Madrid, l'Asie ou l'Amérique.*[17] Because of a reading too narcissistic or empathetic, these sentences will give a new shape to my failings in Valencia, they'll rekindle my memories and gift me the desire, the need, to write about these times out of the house on the basis of this exact experience that unsettled me for a long time and of which I'm still ashamed, this time in Valencia and the obvious fact its failure forced me to face: *from now on, my dwelling also houses my depression, a house within a house.*

Annie Perreault
La femme de Valence

I wordlessly bang my head on the frame, I lose count, se me olvidan las palabras—my syntax fails me like sleep. So I attempt a bit of light. At the window, I place my reflection beneath the floodlights, but the same darkness crops up before me: the night outside, my sunken eyes, my opaque body. So I attempt a bit of clarity: with the tip of my finger on the pane of glass, I draw out my outline, go over the edge a bit. It makes up new streams and a new path, an ersatz of night, of endless promises for words and images for tomorrow. I tremble at the thought of it, with an ailing joy that'll keep me awake for hours; it's terror and ecstasy, this convulsive delight leading me to the end of the road—¿noche enterna o madrugada? I attempt a bit of hope, I say *let's see tomorrow if the battle will be.*

TO CREATE—to get out of the house, to move, to get out of one's self, engage in new loops, in spirals that shift us and associate us with a broader inheritance. *Through creative engagements, you embed your experiences in a larger frame of reference, connecting your personal struggles with those of other beings on the planet, with the struggles of the Earth itself.* To create is to move even beyond people and to dare to seek out bonds of, say, a spiritual nature: depression isn't just an illness, not just a personal struggle, not just a social epidemic. Moreover, even its name, depression, is a poor fit: I've called it *pain, suffering, hurt, anxiety, melancholy.* Depression also in relation with other beings and things around us, a sensitive and parallel knowledge which, thanks to our imaginaries, imbues our vision of the world with the potential for change and for more radical departures from the self. *Imagination links us with what lives outside of us. […] Imagination offers resolutions out of the conflict by dreaming alternative ways of imaging/ feeling/thinking. For positive social change to happen we need to envision a different reality, dream new blueprints for it, formulate new strategies for coping in it.* When we survive it, where it doesn't kill us, depression is one of those experiences that enables us to imagine new ways of shaping a kinder world, because depression holds the potential to recast itself into a multitude of remainders, to

Anzaldúa
"Now let us shift...
the path of conocimiento...
inner work, public acts"

Anzaldúa
"Counsels from the firing...
past, present, future"

grow old within us like traces of a crossing and liberation that modify our relationship to the world and transform the acuity of our gaze. It makes us more sensitive to the unutterable, to the hidden, and this new perceptiveness, what Gloria Anzaldúa calls un conocimiento, in turn shifts, makes possible, even indispensable, the act of creating—never have I been as creative as I've been since the end of this depression, never have I thought of creating with such engagement because creating, once we've freed ourselves of so great a hold, becomes a social engagement and a form of life that enables us to receive the world (the whole of the world: others, things, and everything we can't see) with such a clarity that even simply observing it becomes a political gesture that publicly questions the place that we (humans among objects and abstract things, humans among humans,

Anzaldúa
"Now let us shift..."

spectres and ghosts) occupy in the world. *Breaking out of your mental and emotional prison and deepening the range of perception enables you to link inner reflection and vision— the mental, emotional, instinctive, imaginal, spiritual, and subtle bodily awareness—with social, political action and lived experiences to generate subversive knowledges. These conocimientos challenge official and conventional ways of looking at the world.* To create so that depression (and myself) may be held at a distance (from each other), to observe the creative processes that depression produced by cutting me off from conventional gazes, binary gazes, by linking the intimate and the social, affect and intellect, fiction and truth, ignorance and knowledge, sadness

and joy, poetry and prose, image and speech, the inside

and outside of our houses. With these movements, the body and the pen bring a plural syntax of alternative knowledges into being, one which allows us to know the world better, to know ourselves better, to better love daybreak and this sun obstinately piercing the curtain with its brazen rays.

The way I remember it, fear and shame eclipse everything else on the way to the psychiatrist's office. Fear and shame: major relics of the illness, ones I'm still trying to figure out with my stories.

The way I remember it, my insurer requires an official report signed by one of their psychiatrists in order to confirm the end of my leave of absence, without which I may have to reimburse all the money paid out to me during my sick leave. On the way there, anger wells up inside me, shields me from the fear and shame, keeps me from collapsing on the downtown street, and I give this anger free rein to hold back my tears until I'm in front of the psychiatrist: then I'll let go of the anger to burst into such massive sobs in front of him that he'll have no choice but to sign off on his report and leave me alone once and for all. I muse to myself that the after-effects of my depression are weapons of mass destruction, but of course I know I'm wrong: fear and shame will only ever manage to destroy me in secret, won't ever make a kamikaze out of me.

The way I remember it, the psychiatrist looks like a car salesman: too much gel in his thinning hair, too busy a tie pattern, too many rings on his fingers, too much assurance in his voice, but unlike a car salesman, he doesn't look me in the eye, makes no attempt to reassure me. He says *I don't work for you, I work for the insurance company*. He says *I won't be giving you the report, I'll be giving it to the insurer*. He says *your insurance is good, consider yourself lucky*. He says *I don't want the details, I want the big picture*. He says *I might cut you off, there are details it's crucial for me to include in the report*. He says *this procedure gives me a lot of power, but it's still just a procedure, so let's get on with it*. He stops talking, he doesn't ask any questions, he's just there, pen in hand, notepad on his knee up against the edge of his desk, his chair balanced on its two back legs; I want him to fall backward, I understand the time has come for me to tell him my story.

The way I remember it, fear and shame remain shielded behind the anger that still won't leave me. It gives me a determined look, and this sudden nerve enables me to tell my story in order, from beginning to end, and with a clear, appropriate pace, with a clinical, precise, varied vocabulary, but in so doing I no longer recognize myself: the anecdotes, the reported speech, the symptoms and treatments become abstract within this tale's boring, traditional chronology perfectly constructed for this psychiatric procedure, for this report intended for an insurance company which, this whole time, the whole length of my illness, has only received forms and invoices. This story I tell the psychiatrist is not mine, it belongs to a system that has never not excluded me as a subject.

And as proof: in this story told to the psychiatrist, I never mentioned getting out of the house.

The way I remember it, the meeting ends abruptly, with a *stop, I have everything I need.* In the elevator, I tell myself *that wasn't it, that wasn't my depression. That's not how you tell its story.*

The way I remember it, I step outside, onto the asphalt, sandwiched between two buildings. The anger falls away, I can feel it slip like a weapon dropped. The battle has been, yet still I tell myself *the battle will be.* This is where I collapse.

Endnotes

1 "In asymbolia, in loss of meaning: if I am no longer capable of translating or metaphorizing, I become silent and I die." (Julia Kristeva, *Black Sun: Depression and melancholia*, tr. by Leon S. Roudiez, Columbia University Press, 1989)

2 "Every corner in a house, every angle in a room, every inch of secluded space in which we like to hide, or withdraw into ourselves, is a symbol of solitude for the imagination; that is to say, it is the germ of a room, or of a house." (Gaston Bachelard, *Poetics of Space*, tr. by Maria Jolas, Beacon Press, 1969)

3 "A beautiful façade carved out of a 'foreign language.'" (Ibid.)

4 "In a chain reaction, it shrinks into a morbid loop summed up by the absurd tautology: I suffer because I am suffering." (David Bradford's translation—no translation available.)

5 "My former allies, these thousands of words frantically assembled, had become my prison: the rigidity of what I deduced put up screens all around me." (tr. by D.B.)

6 "The loop tends to complete itself, or the two ends of the tunnel meet up, the nightmares of the day—certain days—visiting those of the night." (tr. by D.B.)

7 "At the heart of the voice." (*Black Sun: Depression and melancholia*)

8 "What's real time? Please give me a definition." (Tr. by D.B.)

9 "Thirty minutes of non-stop francophone music, a real lunchtime gift, don't you think?" (Tr. by D.B.)

10 "'Cause even boredom / and even the end / don't come here / tell me if I'm wrong / we're in the night / and you're inside me / let's forget our lives / rewrite the story." (Tr. by D.B.)

11　"But tell me goodbye tomorrow / but tell me goodbye on your way down the road　/ go see others I don't care at all / I loved you but this is the end for sure" (Tr. by D.B.)

12　Come on we'll dance / at the bar of suicides / like old times we'll close our eyes / come on let's go dance / at the bar of suicides / let your steps one by one before your eyes align" (Tr. by D.B.)

13　"Let's forget our lives / I promise it's the end / at the bar of suicides." (Tr. by D.B.)

14　"In this drama of intimate geometry, where should one live?" (*Poetics of Space*)

15　"Thus, by approaching the house images with care not to break up the solidarity of memory and imagination, we may hope to make others feel all the psychological elasticity of an image that moves us at an unimaginable depth. Through poems, perhaps more than through recollections, we touch the ultimate poetic depth of the space of the house." (*Poetics of Space*)

16　"It's absolutely necessary that we treat this pain, that we nurse it and, especially, that we say it, that we express it. That we face it and acknowledge it: yes, it's you, you squalid, sickly green thing ruining my nights." (Tr. by D.B.)

17　"Claire Halde leaves Valencia without knowing if she'll ever be back. It's an unyielding city, one she has a hard time getting her bearings in, with a layout that belies its seaside location. […] More than any other place in the world, she had managed to lose herself in this city. Even as the train pulls out of the station, she has no concept of north or south, no idea in what direction Barcelona or Madrid, Asia or America lies." (Annie Perreault, *The Woman in Valencia*, tr. Ann Marie Boulanger)

Bibliography

Ahmed, Sara, *The Cultural Politics of Emotion*, Edinburgh, Edinburgh University Press, [2004] 2014.

Anzaldúa, Gloria, "Now let us shift... the path of conocimiento... inner work, public acts," Gloria Anzaldúa and AnaLouise Keating (ed.), *This Bridge Called My Back: Writings by Radical Women of Color*, New York, Routledge, 2002, p. 540-579.

————, "La prieta," Gloria Anzaldúa and Cherríe Morgara (ed.), *This Bridge Called My Back: Writings by Radical Women of Color*, Albany, State University of New York Press, [1981] 2015, p. 198-209.

————, "Counsels from the firing... past, present, future." Foreword to the third edition, 2001. Gloria Anzaldúa and Cherríe Morgara (ed.), *This Bridge Called My Back: Writings by Radical Women of Color*, Albany, State University of New York Press, [1981] 2005, p. 261-266.

Arca, *Arca* [CD], London, XL Recordings, 2017, XLCD834.

Bachelard, Gaston, *La poétique de l'espace*, Paris, Presses universitaires de France, 1957.

————, *The Poetics of Space*, tr. Maria Jolas, Boston, Beacon Press, 1969.

Canaan, Andrea, "Brownness," Gloria Anzaldúa and Cherríe Morgara (ed.), *This Bridge Called My Back: Writings by Radical Women of Color*, Albany, State University of New York Press, [1981] 2015, p. 232-237.

Cheng, Anne Anlin, *The Melancholy of Race: Psychoanalysis, Assimilation, and Hidden Grief*, Oxford, Oxford University Press, 2000.

Curiol, Céline, *Un quinze août à Paris. Histoire d'une dépression*, Arles, Actes Sud, 2014.

Cvetkovich, Ann, *An Archive of Feelings: Trauma, Sexuality, and Lesbian Public Cultures*, Durham, Duke University Press, 2003.

_____, "Public feelings," *South Atlantic Quarterly*, vol. 106, no 3: "After sex? On writing since queer theory," 2007, p. 459-468.

_____, *Depression: A Public Feeling*, Durham, Duke University Press, 2012.

Danquah, Meri Nana-Ama, "Writing the wrongs of identity," Nell Casey (ed.), *Unholy Ghost. Writers on Depression*, New York, HarperCollins Publishers, 2011, p. 173-180.

Eng, David L., and Han, Shinhee, "A dialogue on racial melancholia," *Psychoanalytic Dialogues*, vol. 10, no 4, 2000, p. 667-700.

Hustvedt, Siri, *The Shaking Woman or A History of My Nerves*, New York, Henry Holt, 2009

Kristeva, Julia, *Soleil noir. Dépression et mélancolie*, Paris, Gallimard, 1987.

_____, *Black Sun: Depression and melancholia*, tr. Leon S. Roudiez. New York: Columbia University Press, 1989.

Labro, Philippe, *Tomber sept fois, se relever huit*, Paris, Gallimard, 2003.

Leroux, Mathieu, *Quelque chose en moi choisit le coup de poing*, Montréal, La Mèche, 2016.

Love, Heather, *Feeling Backward: Loss and the Politics of Queer History*, Cambridge, Harvard University Press, 2007.

Muñoz, José Esteban, "Feeling brown, feeling down: Latina affect, the performativity of race, and the depressive position," *Signs*, vol. 31, no 3: "New feminist theories of visual culture," spring 2006, p. 675-688.

Perreault, Annie, *La femme de Valence*, Québec, Alto, 2018.

Perreault, Annie, *The Woman in Valencia*, trans. Ann Marie Boulanger, Montréal, QC Fiction, 2021.

Rosset, Clément, *Route de nuit. Épisodes cliniques*, Paris, Gallimard, 1999.

Sedgwick, Eve Kosofsky, *A Dialogue on Love*, Boston, Beacon Press, 1999.

Styron, William, *Darkness Visible: A Memoir of Madness*, New York, Vintage, 1992

Acknowledgements

The photo on page 33 presents a detail from *I hope this finds you* by Rebecca O'Keefe (silkcreen print on newsprint), 2010, reproduced with the artist's permission.

The photos on page 42 and 44 present the following works by Marie Samuel Levasseur, respectively, reproduced with the artist's permission:
Boîte noire, monotype (etching, inkjet print, gouache), 2007.
Sans titre, diptych (mixed media on canvas), 2008.

Mélissa Samson and Ariel Savion-Lemieux: you might not know it, but your house among the trees is full of words from this book; thank you for the sanctuary.

My parents: gracias por dejarme escribir nuestras historias, inventarnos vidas, ser copuchento a mi manera.

Caroline Dawson: the aloe didn't make it; I like to believe that because of it, I did.

Maude Levasseur: you're the first one to whom I named my fear. This story starts with you.

Gabrielle Tremblay: because you were waiting for me on the platform, in Paris. Getting out of my house was then, all of the sudden, an experience of solidarity.

Pierre-Luc Landry: time does things well, and patience, too. Thank you for your kindness.

Benoit Jodoin: thank you for building this space for clearheaded sensitivity with me, this space where, together, we no longer struggle; with love, we receive, we perceive, we read each other and create.

Translator's Note

Indeed, this other diaspora, amidst ruptures and dispersals, gathers us together. It was a gift to bring *Désormais, ma demeure* to life in English as I worked alongside it on my own scatterings. It's not just that I recognized the ongoing, the from-now-on, of depression, and the particulate heritage, the situatedness, of certain human movements and subjectivities. It's that I recognized their plaiting together, the relief and rub of languages inhabited by each other, the run-on motion of the landscape of this all-encompassing state, one marked by the personal and cultural, one that comes and hopefully goes but somehow stays—that shines and craters in the distance.

House Within a House was a big step for me as a literary translator, so I feel an urge to declare myself. This translation feels like a hook and stitch, a game of darns and sergers to work away at the seam of something new yet absolutely beholden, indebted, and dependent on the integrity of Nicholas Dawson's weaving, his constructed disarray. All that is held in the balance, the definitely new and the decidedly contingent, and the duality of those responsibilities has been a privilege, sometimes a revelation.

From the moment I began this work with Nicholas, it's been a transparent, at times collaborative process. In a process akin to the multilingual play Nicholas describes and instantiates, together, we talked out patterning his patterns of repetition in English, recurring terms and issues, treatment of French quotations, points of misinterpretation, the careful adjustments particular to English, the background to certain passages and pieces, and much more—beginning with a sample all the way to our review of the first draft of the translation. Thank you, Nicholas, for your trust and openness, for being down to talk it out, for your ample energy and time, for the hook and stitch.

Next, I worked through a number of revisions with Erín Moure. I'm always struck anew by how rare and altering a great editor can be. She told me when we began the editing process that she's easy to disagree with, and I was grateful for such a kind, talkative, worker-bee process for this at times tricky bit of work—someone to go at its big questions, multilingual elements, and expansive style with me, the very things that first drew me to Nicholas's work. Waves and grins to my generous editor Erín, who held me to all of it.

Huge thanks to Alayna Munce and the folks at Brick Books for the backup and trust and sheer excitement in taking these steps forward together.

Thank you to Marie-Julie Flagothier at Triptyque for the warm welcome.

Thank you to the editors of *Brick: A Journal* for their excitement for this work.

Note on the Title

There was a momentary debate between Erín and me about how much to open up the nooks and crannies I might let readers enter here, some of the passages or choices of the original that needed a bit of complicated, creative consideration in English, the important bits that didn't transfer over neatly, that needed mulling over and talking out. One such obvious bit I'll let you into: the title.

Désormais, ma demeure, which appears verbatim in the original—the passage on page 147 that reads "*from now on, my dwelling also houses my depression*"—doesn't have an obvious, solid counterpart in English. There's an elevation to the language; there's a formality to "demeure" that matches but is in further common usage than "dwelling." Similarly, "désormais" is elevated and affected, it carries a poetic, sad-ish resolve, but it's still common enough and not that conspicuous, whereas it's most direct translation in English, "henceforth," belongs in restoration theatre and legal documents. What's more, given that *Désormais, ma demeure*'s text employs both "désormais" and "demeure" anaphorically, choosing between permutations of *Henceforth / Hereafter / From Now on / And Now, My Dwelling / Home / Place / Residence* not only reaped bad titles—*Henceforth, My Residence* is maybe the worst, but really, they're all bad—it also threatened a rippling effect. Whereas "désormais," for one, is contextually appropriate in a wide range of passages in the original, no English word was a good translation for all instances in the text; often the best choice was "from now on," sometimes just "now," occasionally "no longer," and in some instances nothing at all. (I won't recount my failed dalliance with "meanwhile" here.)

So, I turned to a number of other title options—okay ones, other bad ones, good ones but for something else—while looking for a title that would have a similar connection to the motif of the "dwelling" and resolve of "désormais." I was drawn to another, quieter bit of repetition in the book: the house. Getting out of it, recounting the times out of it, getting back to it, and then that early passage about the photo hiding in the computer, the situatedness of "a corner turned refuge, a house within a house." *House Within a House*. Which, Nicholas later told me, in a café off Papineau Avenue, months after we had our conversations about finding the right title: he really didn't like at first. But hashing it out, along with the other titles you will not be seeing, Erín and I agreed, and kept agreeing. The title stayed with us through the work. The title grew on Nicholas. And a person who overheard it at the café, a budding writer themself, matter-of-factly declared their love for it (the way I remember it) before popping out. And so, from now on, *House Within a House*—which found its way, with Nicholas's blessing, into my translation of the *"désormais, ma demeure"* passage—would be the title. Hope you feel at home with it too.

Photo: Cedric Trahan

Born in Chile and based in Montréal, **Nicholas Dawson** is a writer, scholar, and the Literary Director of Éditions Triptyque. He is the author of *La déposition des chemins* (La Peuplade, 2010), *Animitas* (La Mèche, 2017), and *Désormais, ma demeure* (Triptyque, 2020), for which he received the Grand Prix du livre de Montréal and the Blue Metropolis Diversity Prize. He is also the co-author of *Nous sommes un continent. Correspondance mestiza* (Triptyque, 2021, with Karine Rosso), and the editor of many anthologies.

Photo: Sarah Bodri

David Bradford is a poet, translator, and editor based in Tio'tia:ke (Verdun). His first book, *Dream of No One but Myself*, won the A.M. Klein Prize for Poetry and was a finalist for the Griffin Poetry Prize, Governor General Literary Awards, and the Gerard Lampert Memorial Award. His forthcoming collection, *Bottom Rail on Top*, will be published in 2023. *House Within a House* is his first book-length translation.